Slave Girl
Return to Hell

Slave Girl
Return to Hell

Ordinary British girls are being sold into sex
slavery; I escaped, but now I'm going back
to help free them. This is my true story.

SARAH FORSYTH WITH TIM TATE

JOHN BLAKE

Published by John Blake Publishing Ltd,
3 Bramber Court, 2 Bramber Road,
London W14 9PB, England

www.johnblakepublishing.co.uk

www.facebook.com/Johnblakepub facebook
twitter.com/johnblakepub twitter

First published in paperback in 2013

ISBN: 978 1 78219 226 8

British Library Cataloguing-in-Publication Data:

A catalogue record for this book is available from the British Library.

Design by www.envydesign.co.uk

Printed and bound in Great Britain by CPI Group (UK) Ltd

3 5 7 9 10 8 6 4 2

Papers used by John Blake Publishing are natural, recyclable
products made from wood grown in sustainable forests.
The manufacturing processes conform to the
environmental regulations of the country of origin.

Every attempt has been made to contact the relevant copyright-
holders, but some were unobtainable. We would be grateful if the
appropriate people could contact us.

This book is dedicated to victims of sex trafficking and sex slavery, wherever they are in the world. It is also dedicated to the brave men and women who devote their lives to fighting this modern evil.

INTRODUCTION

FOREWORD

This book began with an email and a letter.

The email came from a reader of *Slave Girl*, the book which told Sarah Forsyth's story of being tricked into international sex slavery and her difficult, often flawed, struggle to break free of its tentacles. Had we, the email asked, stopped to look at the wider picture? Did we know that there are, by even conservative estimates, 27 million slaves in the world today – more than twice the number of men, women and children who were snatched and transported from Africa over the entire 350 years of the historic international slave trade?

The answers were – to my shame – no on both counts: I had no idea that slavery still existed, let alone on such a vast scale. Surely it had been abolished more than 250 years ago? So, who were these men and women? Where were they? How did they end up in slavery – and what was the nature of their enslavement? And, in a world where slavery is illegal in every country on the planet, how on earth could this be possible?

Those unanswered questions led me to devote an entire year of my working life to investigating modern slavery in all its forms. Not 'slave-labour wages', as lazy journalism often tags the undoubted exploitation of low-paid workforces, but real, genuine slavery: human beings held against their will, forced to work for no pay and threatened, beaten or even killed if they attempt to leave.

The result was an eight-part documentary series, *Slavery: A 21st Century Evil*, broadcast throughout the world, which told the stories of modern slaves in countries as diverse as Brazil, Pakistan, India, Haiti, Thailand and China. But it was not these sometimes remote places which held the greatest surprise: slavery, after all, has always been ineluctably intertwined with poverty – endemic in the slums of Haiti or the remote villages of Southeast Asia. It was the existence – no, the thriving – of slavery in rich, developed nations of the so-called First World, which was most disturbing. And disturbing not simply because America, Holland and Great Britain had led the way in abolishing the historic slave trade 200 years ago (indeed, the United States had torn itself apart throughout four terrible years of civil war to fight for the emancipation of slaves): what really hit home was the stark fact that it is all of us in the industrialised West who are, to a large extent, driving modern slavery. We are each of us, in effect, slave-masters.

The instinctive response to such a shocking proposition is, not unnaturally, to deny it: when it was first put to me I experienced a momentary indignation at the very idea. The most I was prepared to concede was that if it were in any way true, then I was ignorant of it – and therefore innocent of any culpability. In truth, there is some justification in that argument. None of us would knowingly support or condone slavery, but the evidence is remarkably clear that as consumers we use or benefit from the forced labour of slaves. From the cars we drive to the technology we take for granted, slave-made products taint the most common place goods and services we enjoy. So why don't we know about it? Of course manufacturers – and even some countries – work hard to disguise the slave-origins of their products: can we be expected to do diligent research on each and every item we buy to ensure it is free of forced labour?

We try to answer that difficult question at the end of this book but there is one type of 21st-century slavery for which we have no excuse of reasonable ignorance. Its victims are visible – in some countries highly visible indeed – to anyone who walks down a suburban high street or city alleyway.

Sex slavery accounts, by most estimates, for between six and eight per cent of the 27 million men, women and children held as slaves today. Often campaigners, journalists and filmmakers preface that statistic with the word 'just' – 'just six to eight per cent'. I have been as guilty of this as most – and for, I like to think, a perfectly sensible reason. Sex slavery has overly dominated the agenda of those who fight to free modern slaves. As one campaigner put it, 'Sex is, well, sexy – even when it isn't. We know we can get headlines from stories about sex slavery – and if that's what it takes to raise people's consciousness about the whole issue, then I guess it's a price worth paying.' But, however small a percentage of the total, the maths of sex slavery means that today, right now – whenever you pick up this book – there are almost two million people forced to work as prostitutes. Two million. Two million men women and children – that's more than the entire population of Edinburgh, Birmingham and Glasgow put together – who on any given day are being held against their will and made to sell sexual services.

Do we not know this? Are these human beings somehow out of sight? Of course not. We know but we choose not to think about it.

The letter arrived while I was making the slavery series. It was from Sarah, and it spoke for itself.

Tim Tate
November 2012

Gateshead
Tyne & Wear
September 2011

Hello Tim

I thought it was about time I wrote and apologised for my terrible behaviour you had to endure while working with me on our book.

From what I can remember – and believe me that's not a lot – I know I must have been awful. I have only vague recollections of that time: the drugs I was prescribed and the alcohol I was addicted to made me act in a way that I am ashamed of. My marriage was falling apart and I know I made life difficult for everyone around me: my family, you – and me. Truly, I am so sorry.

A lot has happened since then. I am finally free of drink and drugs – even the medication I was taking. I am no longer addicted to anything and, for once in my life, I am in total control.

I am divorced now and have pulled free of people who can hurt me or drag me back to the dark place where I was when we last met. I have a beautiful flat, where I live on my own with a little dog, and I see my mum almost every day. We never go a day without talking and life feels amazing.

What's more, something you would never have guessed has happened – I am working. I never thought I would be able to work ever again, but now I have a job – and not just an ordinary job either. I have trained as an addictions counsellor and am helping with a local charity, which supports people like I used to be.

They recognise that with all I have been through I have both sympathy and empathy with their clients. I see them and know that I have been where they are; but more importantly, they see me and know I have been in their situation and managed to come out the other side.

It feels so good to be helping somebody else at last, especially after all that everyone did for me, which brings me to the other reason to write to you.

I feel so lucky to have escaped from the sex industry. How many women like me has it consumed: ensnared, chewed up, spat out? How many women this very day and this very moment are still trapped within it – in Britain, in the Netherlands, anywhere, somewhere in towns and cities across the world?

To this day I can't remember how long I was forced to rent out my body in Amsterdam's red-light windows but I can't forget the pain. Every hour felt like a day; every day felt like a week. And the weeks turned into months, with only the false friends of cocaine, crack and cannabis to hold my hand and see me through the endless treadmill of men's selfish lust.

And I feel guilty. Guilty because I survived. Guilty because I got out. Guilty because there are so many other Sarah Forsyths still there. They are the slaves I left behind, and I can't get them out of my head.

So, Tim, is there something we can do to change that? So many readers of our book have written with such kindness: they have given me the strength I need to be who I now am. But there are countless women like me who need that support right now. Is there some way we could together do something – anything – to give them help?

What do you think?

Love, Sarah

INTRODUCTION

It was the photographs. Three of them, in a little row like a short clip of celluloid film or the frames of a comic strip. But there was nothing humorous about them, nothing of entertainment in the story they told. And it was a story I knew only too well to ignore.

The first was cut from the tape of a closed-circuit television camera at Schiphol airport in Amsterdam. It was in four quarters, each picture capturing a few seconds of action in the middle of the concourse between B and D departure gates.

In the first shot of the sequence a man – a big, burly shaven-headed man – approaches a slight, blonde-haired woman in a pink top, jeans and flat ballet-pump shoes. She is at least a foot shorter and many stones lighter than him. A split second later, the next frame captures him reaching out to grab her arms; her hands are raised as she tries to fend him off. Cut to frame three: he has hold of her wrists; her back arches as she tries to pull away from him. The final image is of him wrestling with her: the pink top has pulled up, exposing her lower back as she struggles with her assailant. A young man – a bystander – wanders past, seemingly oblivious to the drama happening less than three feet away.

My mind shutters back across 15 years. I know this concourse: it was my gateway to Hell and – eventually – the first steps on my faltering path to freedom. But there will be no freedom for the young girl in the photos: I know that as surely as I know what is happening in the photos.

The image is blurred and grainy, as CCTV footage always is. Even so, it is clear that this is a young woman – no more than a girl, really – and she is trying to get away from a man who has enslaved her – or who is trying to do so.

The next picture was taken a day or so later at a police station. It is a classic single-frame mugshot, its banality reinforced by the unforgiving lighting of a sodium strip light reflected on the white ceramic tiles on the walls. The eyes of its subject stare back at me, vacant and almost lifeless. But this is not the mugshot of a man taken in custody, and the eyes are not those of a suspect: this is a photograph of the young girl at the airport.

Her eyes gaze into mine. I notice they are brown, like mine. But beneath each of them are large and livid bruises, still a fresh red-colour where the blood has flushed to the skin. She has very recently been punched and beaten.

And then the final photograph. The girl has turned

round – or been turned round: her back is to the camera and her top pulled up, almost as if the police were recreating the final frame of the CCTV footage. But this is not the reason: the photographer is capturing a tattoo scrolled across her skin, just above the swell where her buttocks begin.

At first glance it resembles the antlers that many young girls have engraved on their lower backs. But look closer: in the centre of these antlers, cupped in the horn, a word – 'Abu'. I know with a terrible certainty what this tattoo means; I have known it at first hand and for 15 long and painful years.

This is not a tattoo but a brand; it signifies the girl is owned. Her master has put his mark on her – he is a trafficker, she is a sex slave.[1] The photographs do not lie, nor will they allow me to avoid the truth any longer. When last you met me I wrote these words:

My name is Sarah Forsyth. I was an abused child and a sex slave. I was a trafficked woman and a crack whore. I am many things: some good, some bad. I am weakness and I am strength. I am fear and I am love. I am despair and I am hope. But I am one thing above all else: I am a survivor.

All of this was – *is* – true, although there is so much more to tell about my journey between Hell and the upper world. But there is something else I am, or have become. Survivors bear a duty: a duty, yes, to speak of their ordeal, but a much greater responsibility to do something about it.

This will be a journey every bit as hard as my escape from sex slavery but it is one I must make for the sake of those who remain trapped in it.

Will you make it with me?

---

[1] In case any reader should doubt Sarah's account, Dutch police and prosecutors confirm it to the letter. The young woman in the photographs was indeed tattooed by the man seen wrestling with her. He ran a multi-national trafficking enterprise, with each of 'his' women made to carry his brand as if they were cattle.

CHAPTER ONE

THE NINE CIRCLES OF HELL

How do you describe Hell?

Go on: try. I have been asked – am still asked, constantly – to describe what I have been through. People who knew me once, a long time ago and in another world, ask me: school friends perhaps, or members of the family I lost. People who never knew me until they picked up my book and read about things they had never thought could happen; people who have never read the book but have heard about it from friends or neighbours. Everyone asks me: what was it *really* like?

Perhaps they can't quite bring themselves to believe that human beings can treat each other so badly. Some have said that I must have been making it up or exaggerating. Maybe that's why they ask me to describe it over and over again.

And yet the truth is that every time I try it seems impossible to put into words the indelible horror of being forced into the waking nightmare of sex slavery, and chained to the seemingly impossible weight of addiction. Even typing this now the words seem inadequate: 'horror', 'nightmare' – how can such little words convey what it was like just to keep breathing, day after day, week after week, year after year?

So go on: try to describe the worst thing that has ever happened in your life. Force yourself back into your darkest, bleakest time; try to inhabit that memory with all its pain and sorrow and bitterness. And then multiply it: make it bigger and deeper and darker and lonelier than you can bear.

Feel the tears come back until they choke you with sobbing. Pull it around you and over you until you can't breathe and are sure you're going to die. And then you may know a tiny fraction of what it was – still is – like.

Perhaps you think I am being melodramatic or wallowing in self-pity but the truth is that I'm not talking about what I myself have gone through: I'm talking about what millions of other women are going through this very moment, as you read these words. For they are the ones trapped in sex slavery, their voices silenced by fear, their bodies shattered by abuse and degradation. And I am the person on the outside, trying to speak loudly enough to be the voice that has been taken from them, trying to help someone – *anyone* – see enough, care enough to break their bonds.

But I'm getting ahead of myself. We need to start at the beginning and go from there.

The headline was certainly eye-catching: **'SEX SLAVE AND THE NURSE'S HEPATITIS C HELL'**.

Thousands of people must have read it that Sunday morning, perhaps over breakfast or, more likely, given this was the *Sunday Sun* – Newcastle's local weekly tabloid rag – in the pub.[1] What did they think of these casual consumers of other people's misery? The writer had never met me but seemed in no doubt about my wickedness.

'Former sex slave Sara Lee subjected a nurse to a deadly Hepatitis C scare.

'Drug addict Lee was having emergency treatment for an overdose when she became aggressive and abusive and spat in the nurse's mouth. It sparked a terrifying chain of events because both Lee and the nurse knew she had been diagnosed with Hepatitis C. And for months the nurse had to undergo screening and live with the threat she had become infected. Lee was jailed for 38 days by Gateshead magistrates after admitting common assault. But the 33-year-old, from Duke Walk, Teams, Gateshead, walked free from court because she has already spent 27 days in custody on remand at Low Newton Prison waiting for the case to be heard. She was, though, ordered to pay the victim £250 from royalties she is expecting this month for her book, *Slave Girl*.'

I had become a local celebrity. And I couldn't be more ashamed.

The facts, of course, are never as simple or as straightforward as they appear in cold, hard print but they're as good a place as any to start.

Tracy and I had been together for a few months when

we decided that we would get 'married', hence the name Sara Lee in the article. It was a civil partnership of course, not a marriage, but it felt like one in every way: from the flowers in Tracy's buttonhole and clutched tightly in my hands to the exchange of rings and the promises of love everlasting. And when it was over I became Mrs Lee.

But it was like a marriage in other, less happy, ways, too. One in three real marriages ends in divorce and same-sex civil partnerships seem to be heading in the same direction: 4.6 per cent of women like Tracy and I have their unions dissolved and we were destined to be one small, unnoticed fragment of that unhappy statistic.

We fought about everything. God knows, I can't have been easy to live with but then neither was Tracy: two very damaged, vulnerable women, brought together in adversity and clinging to each other – when we weren't arguing and scrapping – in a way that I imagine someone who is drowning snatches at any tiny scrap of flotsam that might keep them afloat.[2]

I rarely spent more than three nights in a row in our claustrophobic first-floor flat. It was a tiny space, filled with as much desperation as smoke from the cigarettes we sucked on for comfort. Three days, three nights were as much as I could bear: I felt I was being smothered, the life force – such as it was – slowly draining out of me. And so I ran.

Where did I run to? Half the time I couldn't tell you. Not to my mum's, that's for sure. She was still wary of me and quite right, too. She'd come to our wedding on that cold clear day in 2007, but she didn't like Tracy and didn't like the way we existed. I say 'existed' because you couldn't call it living, not in the way that real people, people who haven't been damaged in the way we had been live. Not for us the Mills & Boon romance or the happy ever after we'd imagined.

I was still dependent on my methadone: while being weaned off the cocaine and crack I'd been fed in Amsterdam, I'd been put on morphine and had ended up addicted to that instead. Methadone was supposed to be a way of managing the cravings but really it just replaced one bad 'street' drug with another, chemically pure poison.

It poisoned my body, it poisoned my mind, but most of all it poisoned our relationship. Tracy was adamant that I should get myself off it, but it's easier said than done. I needed it to block out the searing pain that I was afraid to confront: the pain of being abused as a child and then re-abused as a sex slave in the Red Light District. And so methadone became the third person in our partnership, and no marriage can survive with three people inside it – especially not if one of the three is as jealous and demanding a lover as methadone.

Sometimes when I ran I would seek out others like me: misery loves company, so the saying goes, and round our way there's plenty of that to go round. Although methadone is prescribed under strict conditions and the little plastic cups of its numbing green liquid are meant to be swallowed by an addict in the presence of the pharmacist who dispenses it, there always seemed to be people selling doses on the streets or in dingy flats, smelling of stale cigarettes and even staler empty cans of super-strong lager. Perfect for someone like me: a real home from home.

Of course I never stayed away for long. Something – maybe the need for someone special to hold, maybe the hope that love could be possible for Sarah Forsyth – always sent me back to Tracy and my legal status as Mrs Lee, her wife. Guilt, too, played its part: I'd made a promise in that Register Office and I'd made a home – of sorts – in our little flat. It was first time in more than 15 years that I'd tried to make a home and I wanted so much to make it work. Maybe if I tried harder next time I could make it all alright. But there was a next time, and another next time and countless more after that. The same old tawdry pattern of arguments, running away and drowning my sorrows in the company of those just as lonely, damaged and desperate as me.

Does that sound like self-pity? I hope not because it was thanks to this miserable routine that I finally began to heal. But being me, that healing had to begin with a very physical wound.

I was in a pub – not exactly an unusual occurrence in those days. It was one of the times when I had run away and I lost myself in booze. Somehow a fight began: a raised voice, an argument, a glass snatched, smashed and thrust at my face. I ducked but the jagged edge of the broken glass caught me on the side of my head. Blood poured faster than I thought it could; the pub went from vicious noise to shocked silence. Someone pointed at me and yelled for the staff to call an ambulance: my left ear was hanging from the side of my face, attached only by a sliver of skin.

Flashing lights. Hospital corridors. A & E. I was weak from the loss of blood and almost delirious. Even so I remember thinking, 'Has it really come to this? Have I got this far, got away from Amsterdam, escaped the clutches of my traffickers, only to bleed to death from a random fight in a grubby pub, full of sad and broken fellow addicts?'

They sewed my ear back on: stitch after shameful stitch, a physical mark of how low I'd fallen there for everyone to see. And they kept me in overnight for observation. But that night I was the one doing the observation: I looked at myself and I saw what I had become – and I hated it. I hated me, I hated my marriage, and I hated my addiction. There in that hospital bed I saw that I had hit rock bottom: I had sunk even further and deeper than when I was behind those neon-lit windows in Amsterdam. That Sarah didn't have a choice but this one did, and I was determined to make it.

It sounds easy when I put it like that. But it wasn't, not by a long chalk.

The next day a social worker rang my mum to tell her that I was being taken away from Gateshead to a sort of safe house. My poor mum. She must have been wondering if this would ever end: the first time she'd seen me after I escaped from the Red Light District I was in a safe house somewhere in Holland, under police protection from sex traffickers. 12 years on and I was being carted off to another one by social workers, worried about a bunch of violent drug addicts.

Knowing Mum, she must have been feeling a whole contradictory range of emotions: relief that I was being taken away from all the influences she thought were bad for me, but fear I was slipping back into my old, self-destructive ways. Anger that her life was once again being turned upside down by her wayward daughter, but hope that this time, please this time, it would be the start of a new beginning. Or something like it.

The safe house turned out to be a lovely little place on the coast. Whitley Bay is no more than 10 miles from Gateshead but it felt like a world away. Once upon a time it was a favourite holiday destination for working people from all across the Northeast. It has a wonderful long sandy beach, stretching from St Mary's Island in the north to Cullercoats in the south. Its other chief claim to fame was Spanish City – a permanent funfair built to rival Blackpool's Pleasure Beach. Dire Straits immortalised it in their hit song 'Tunnel Of Love' – which was played every morning until the whole park closed down in 2002.

Everyone from Gateshead knew the Spanish City: most of us had been there – or dreamed of going there – as kids. But now as I walked up and down the golden sands I didn't miss it: I was just so relieved to be free, in a place where no one knew me and I wasn't surrounded by the sad and desperate people I had called my friends.

I stayed in Whitley Bay for two months. It was here that I took the first faltering steps on what would turn out to be my ultimate – if meandering – road to recovery. Mum came to see me as often as she could get time away from work, and I began a pattern of skipping days of collecting and drinking my shot of methadone. At the time I thought it was good idea: I hated queuing up with other addicts, waiting for the chemist to hand over the little plastic beaker of 'normality'. But, as it turned out, it proved to be both good and bad in equal measures.

At the end of two months, I was ready to leave the safety of the little house on the windy coastline but where would I go? I couldn't – *wouldn't* – go home to Tracy, and I didn't want to slip back into the shadowy world of my old addict acquaintances.

It took me a few days but then I remembered an old, old friend who had been good and true and supportive of me in the years between Amsterdam and Tracy: Eddie. Of course, I'd go and stay with Eddie.

I owe Eddie more than I can ever tell him. If you're reading this, Eddie: you were a huge part of my recovery, one of the first and most vital of foundations on which I finally built a life. Thank you, old friend – thank you.

Eddie also lived in Gateshead, but in a much nicer, less grubby part of town than me. There had never been anything between us romantically, much less sexually, but I knew I could trust him with my life. And that's exactly what I did.

For the very first time I had a taste of normality – real life as it's lived by normal people. There were no drugs and even though he enjoyed a drink like most normal people, Eddie never, ever, in the year I stayed with him brought alcohol into the house. This was a first for me: with Tracy there was always beer – strong stuff – and I always kept a bottle of vodka handy. With Eddie there was no booze around me, and I began to feel that I might one day be able to do without it.

My doctor also began reassessing my medication. For the past 12 years I'd been on diazepam – known to most people by its trade name of Valium. It's a powerful anti-depressant and was given to me to control the anxiety and panic attacks I still suffered as a result of what had happened in Amsterdam. Valium is also used to help alcoholics kick the drink – but if that was ever considered for me then I'd done a pretty good job of boozing and pill popping at the same time.

Gradually the doctor reduced my dosage, taking me down in stages so that my body could understand the process and readjust. It's the classic way of coming off any addictive medication – and diazepam is very addictive indeed, especially if you've been on it as long as I had. And slowly but surely, my body did come to terms with less and less diazepam. But my mind – well, that's a whole different story.

At this point I started to suffer from anxiety and spasmodic panic attacks; the memories of everything I'd been through would suddenly flood into my mind and drown out everything else. I began to see the faces of people I had seen walking by the windows in Amsterdam, staring back at me now just as they had stared at me as I posed and pirouetted, desperately trying to lure them into my little corner of Hell so that I could keep up the flow of money my pimps demanded of me every single day.

People today can't believe that I could have noticed these faces; but I did, oh I did. Old faces, young faces, sad faces, happy faces... I stood there every day and every night in that neon-lit glass prison with nothing else to do but look out and try and hook them. Half of me was desperate to find the next customer – fearful as I was of the beatings that would come my way if I didn't meet my quota of clients – while the other half was, I think, searching for a face in the crowd that might, just might, be someone with enough spark of humanity to see how wretched I was and somehow do something to put an end to it.

So, yes, I saw and remembered the faces, and now, as my body adjusted to ever-lower doses of the anti-depressant, my mind conjured them back up to stare back at me and haunt my waking hours with the searing pain of traffic that had passed by me and sometimes through me.

Does that describe Hell? No, it describes just one of its circles. According to literature, Hell consists of nine circles of suffering, all located within the earth.[3] By now, I was going through every single one of them.

I was still on methadone, of course: 60 milligrams of the magic green liquid every day. There are a lot of misconceptions about methadone: people think that it's a cure for addiction to heroin or other opiate drugs but it isn't, and it never has been. In fact it was developed in Nazi Germany in 1937 because the country needed a steady supply of opiates and the way the world was then – and the way it would go two years later when war broke out and hundreds of thousands of soldiers would need quick shots of very powerful painkillers on the battlefield – traditional supplies of opium poppies were just not reliable, so German chemists invented a synthetic version that they could create in large quantities very quickly. Methadone was born.

Since the end of World War II it has been used to 'treat' addiction to opiate drugs – either servicemen who became dependent on morphine or junkies hooked on street heroin. But 'treat' is really the wrong word: all it does is replace often dodgy or dirty illegal drugs with a carefully controlled and scientifically pure alternative. And here's the big problem: it doesn't get you off drugs. People – and I was one of them – stay on methadone for decades without ever solving the real cause of their addiction.

Of course, doctors and governments are doing this for the best possible reason: street drugs, bought from a dealer most likely hooked himself, are cut with everything from talcum powder to rat poison – not exactly guaranteed to help a body already ravaged by addiction. And of course many junkies shoot up their little wrap of smack using dirty needles: HIV and Hepatitis C are almost always the inevitable result.

The best way to make methadone work as a method of helping an addict get clean is to put them on a carefully monitored reduction programme, taking the doses down little by little. Over two or three years, my doctors had got me on a programme that had cut down my daily dose from 120 milligrams to 60 milligrams. The programme had been working so well that I suppose I became a bit over-confident. I'd started missing out days when I was staying in the little house in Whitley Bay. Now that I was back in Gateshead I'd sometimes go several days without getting my dose, hoping that I could speed the whole process along with willpower.

I knew full well that coming off medication wasn't going to be easy but I had made up my mind that if I was going to have any sort of a normal life then I would just have to be strong and do it. But God, did it take willpower. Even a couple of days without my 'scrip' (as junkies call prescriptions) and I would get the dreaded 'methadone rattle'.

One of the bitter ironies of methadone is that the withdrawal symptoms are far worse than those for heroin or morphine: far, far more painful and they last much longer – often for weeks on end. Vomiting, diarrhoea, sweating, stomach cramps, headaches, irregular heartbeat, hallucinations, delirium, paranoia and panic attacks – that's the standard recipe for the methadone rattle. And I went through every single one of its ingredients.

At some point I knew I'd had enough and had pushed myself too far, too fast. I had wanted to be clean so much that I'd detoxed far too quickly. And so I went to the clinic to get my methadone. My appointment was for 4.30 in the afternoon but I was so desperate that I set off and got there more than two hours early.

I was in pretty bad state when I arrived – shaking, crying, with every bone in my whole body aching. But the clinic wouldn't see me early: they're pretty strict – rightly so, I know – about appointments and I was told that I'd just have to take my turn and wait. I didn't know what to do with myself: two more hours of the terrible agony and convulsions seemed an eternity.

As usual there was a small crowd outside the clinic: other addicts who'd just had their methadone or were waiting to get it. And, as usual, there were 'friends' there, offering to help by selling an extra or top-up dose.

Even giving away a dose of your methadone – much less selling it – is against the law. But then what did the law matter to those already addicted to illegal drugs? Before I really knew what was happening someone had seen me – and seen me 'rattling' badly – and dosed me with 'spare' methadone.

Just my bad luck. The stuff they gave me was a far higher dosage than I'd been on for the past few years. My body reacted very quickly: I found that I couldn't breathe, my blood pressure dropped, my skin became cold and clammy, my muscles went into spasm and I spun off into a dizzying faint. Someone must have rushed into the clinic and told them. I was just about unconscious and I don't remember anything about it but the doctors went to work to stop me drifting into a coma. Apparently they gave me a much-needed injection of adrenaline to bring me back to consciousness.

The first thing I can remember is a nurse's face very close to mine – and throwing up all over her. Some of my bile and vomit flew into her mouth.

I was mortified: how low could I get? Collapsing outside a drug clinic after an overdose, then splattering sick over one of the very people who dedicated their lives to helping others like me? But it was far worse than I thought – much, much worse, as it turned out.

The clinic thought I'd done it deliberately – that I'd purposely spat at the nurse in a fit of anger. Of course I hadn't, but woozy and disoriented I struggled to explain what had really happened. Someone called the police. I was arrested and charged with common assault. Following

THE NINE CIRCLES OF HELL

this, I was held in custody and spent 27 days on remand at Low Newton Prison waiting for my case to be heard.

How do I describe what was going through my head? I'd tried so hard to get clear of the trouble in my life – I'd split up with Tracy, moved away from my old haunts and pubs full of addicts and alcoholics, yet here I was in prison again.[4]

I thought of my mum and the terrible shame I had once more brought on her and on my family. And I thought of all the people who had said such positive, uplifting things about me after my book was published, but most of all I thought about the nurse I'd been sick over.

A few months before I'd been told by my doctor that I was suffering from Hepatitis C. It's a viral infection – and a really nasty one at that – which attacks the liver and can cause cirrhosis. Sometimes those who contract the illness can die of liver failure or cancer. Hepatitis C is generally transmitted through the blood but in some cases it may be passed on through other fluids such as spit or vomit.

Locked in my cell at Low Newton no one told me that the nurse I'd thrown up over was going through a whole series of tests to check that I hadn't infected her, but then I didn't really need telling. After all, I had plenty of time to think about what I'd done – albeit inadvertently – and what it might mean. And that's when I came to the real rock bottom.

Someone – a drug and alcohol addictions counsellor, I think – once told me that to really begin the process of change every addict has to come to a point so low, so debased and so terrible that they realise something must change. It may be a cliché but it really is true that when you're right at the bottom, the only way is up. And there, in that shameful prison, I made a solemn promise: this time I was going to do it. Once and for all, I was going to break free.

I was taken before Gateshead magistrates in September 2009. After I pleaded guilty to the one charge of common assault, the prosecution outlined its case and explained how the agony of worrying about what I'd done had affected the nurse. Then my solicitor explained my side of the story. When everyone had had their say the court handed down its sentence: 38 days in prison.

But I'd already served 27 days on remand and the magistrates must have taken pity on me because they decided not to send me back for the remaining 11 days. A feeling of relief flooded through me. I was never officially told what happened to the nurse but news reached me on the grapevine that – thankfully – the tests had come back negative: I hadn't passed on my Hepatitis C.

I don't think I ever got to apologise to her properly: I very much wanted to do so but the whole formal business of police and courts seemed to get in the way of any chance of doing so. Perhaps, if you're reading this, you'll let me tell you now that I am truly sorry: I never meant it to happen and I would never deliberately put another human being through such trauma. Please believe me when I tell you how sorry I am.

As soon as I was released from the court, I made my way outside to find Mum. It must have been awful for her to sit through all the evidence and have our family's dirty linen once again aired in public. But she did. And she waited for me, and she hugged me and I told her that it would never happen again.

Did she believe me? She wanted to, that much I do know – but how could she really?

---

1 The *Sunday Sun* in Newcastle is part of the Mirror Group's stable of local newspapers. It has no connection with the national *Sun on Sunday*, which was launched by News International after the closure of the *News of the World*.

2 Like Sarah, Tracy had been in prison and had struggled with substance abuse.

3 Dante's Inferno, described in his epic work, 'The Divine Comedy' (1861–68).

4 Sarah's one previous brush with the Law, not long after she escaped from Amsterdam, had resulted in a jail term for passing a dud cheque and minor shoplifting offences, which lasted several months.

CHAPTER TWO

'THE CHILD OF THOSE TEARS SHALL NEVER PERISH.'

Mum... My poor mum.

When I think of all that she's had to go through in her life, I just don't know how she found the strength to keep on going. Married to an abuser – and a child abuser at that. Divorce, and then Mark – her son, her only son, dying of cancer: who but a mother can know the pain of burying your own child? And her two daughters: one snatched away into sex slavery, drug abuse and now in a seemingly endless circle of recovery then disaster – and the second having moved abroad, partly to get away from the antics of her sister.

It would be enough – more than enough – to break anyone. Yet somehow my mum kept on. Whatever I did, whatever people said about me, I knew she was always there in the background waiting, hoping that I would somehow return to her. All the while she somehow managed to keep the semblance of a family together despite the fact that my sister could barely bring herself to speak my name.

Rachel is younger than me. She's everything, I suppose, I haven't been. She has a great job, a lovely life in New York and has never dragged Mum through the sort of misery that I have over the years. By the time the court had finished with me that day in September we hadn't spoken for years. I know it hurt her – and underneath everything else it was tearing me apart. Mum knew that and somehow kept a sort of dialogue by proxy going between us. She acted as the go-between, telling each of us news of the other and hoping against hope that one day we might actually talk to each other.

She was – and is – my rock. But how on earth did Mum do it?

Well, for one thing she's got a wonderful new husband – my step-dad – who has been by her side through all the terrible years and hasn't argued, complained or walked away. I can only imagine what it means to have someone strong and caring beside you – through the worst times as well as the best. Naturally I envy Mum, but God knows she deserved this.

And, if you asked Mum that would be exactly the phrase: 'God knows'. She's been a Catholic all her life – a real, proper Christian, not one of those 'holier-than-thou' pulpit polishers who condemn with one side of their mouths while smarming out words of forgiveness from the other. No, Mum is what I call a Christian. Someone who tries – succeeds, if you ask me – to follow the things that Jesus taught: love thy neighbour, forgive those who do you harm, but love, always love, above all else.

After my brother Mark died, Mum began quietly saying prayers to him. I was in what I call my lost years then: in and out of prison or police witness protection programmes, swigging vodka like it was water and hanging out with a whole unsavoury crew of equally unprepossessing people. So Mum prayed to Mark to watch over me, to watch over Rachel – over all of us, really.

Now I'm not especially religious. Oh, I believe in God – don't doubt that – but the whole panoply of churches and rituals and fancy robes seems to me to be in the way of a real spiritual life. I do go to church – though not religiously (if you'll excuse the very bad pun) but for me, my relation-ship with God is a quiet and very personal one, best attended to on my own and far away from the smells and bells of traditional Sunday services. Still, maybe I'm wrong because there came a time when Mum's faith seemed to get the results.

By the time I was living in the little house in Whitley Bay she'd shifted the focus of her prayers. Mark was ever-present in them, but he wasn't the person she prayed to. I hope you'll bear with me as I introduce you to the person she started to talk to.

Readers: meet Saint Monica. Saint Monica: meet the readers.

I don't know to this day what made Mum change her chosen prayer-figure, or whether she even knew what made her choose the person she did, but when you look at

Saint Monica's life you'd have to be blind not to see that she's something of a natural for the Forsyth family.

Saint Monica was born in Algeria, 331 years after the birth of Christ. She died in Rome, 56 years later. From shortly afterwards she was an important saint of the early Christian church. Most historians know her as the mother of Saint Augustine of Hippo – a very big noise indeed in the Christian tradition. Other than giving birth to one of Christianity's biggest hitters, Monica is particularly remembered – and venerated – for her outstanding patience with the vile temper and perpetual adulteries of her husband, and her prayerful dedication to the reformation of her son.

Augustine lived an unhealthy part of his early life as a dissolute and wayward reprobate. You'd be hard pushed to find a better example of someone living up to the image of a prodigal son than young Augustine. And it isn't a big stretch in my mind to see in Monica's quietly determined prayers for Augustine my mum's equally long-suffering tears and prayers for me. (Not to mention what she had endure with my dad's brutality and constant tom-catting around town.)

Anyway, at some point Monica apparently went to see a bishop about Augustine and begged him to intervene in the boy's life in order to save it. Mum did the same with me. And she got pretty much the same response as Monica: the bishop couldn't really do anything. But in Monica's case, the bishop sent her away with a phrase that has somehow survived and been passed on for nearly 2,000 years. He told her: 'The child of those tears shall never perish.'

When Mum prayed to Saint Monica that's exactly what came back.

Today, if I ask her about it, Mum is quietly reticent: she just says that she never gave up and that she always knew that with God's help she'd get me back – really, properly forever back – one day. Me, I think it's down to Saint Monica but that's just me. You don't have to believe it if you don't want to. End of sermon.

We went for coffee that morning in September 2009. I looked my mum in the eye and told her that I'd reached a decision and I wasn't going back, even if it killed me.

'I'm going to give myself 12 weeks and in those 12 weeks I'm going to get off this methadone, get clean of drugs and drink and everything, and I'm going to be the daughter you always hoped for.'

Of course she had heard it all before so who could blame her if she took it with a pinch of salt? But I meant it. There was just one little problem.

The thing about Hepatitis C is that it's an old disease that's only recently been identified. Scientists didn't discover the virus that causes it until 1999 – which is probably four years after I was infected. There's no vaccine to protect people and it's alarmingly easy to catch. What's more, most people who have it don't actually know, and yet left untreated it's the main factor in victims needing a liver transplant.

A quick look through the list of famous people who've had the disease showed I was in exalted company: *Baywatch* star Pamela Anderson contracted it from a tattoo done with a shared needle; Anita Roddick, who founded The Body Shop, and the stunt motorbike daredevil Evel Knievel were infected by blood transfusions, but the most common causes are unprotected sex and intravenous drug use.

So, how had I got it? I was pretty certain that however terrible my life as a sex slave had been, I had never had sex with a client without a condom. And though my captors got me hooked on drugs, I don't remember anyone ever injecting me – and I definitely never did. The more I thought about it, the most likely cause was my tattoos. Much to Mum's disquiet I have a lot of ink in my skin. Some of the tattoos are beautiful – I have a lovely flower-chain motif running down my left arm to my wrist – others were a little more basic and I was possibly less careful than I should have been about how and where they were done. In the end all that mattered was that I had Hepatitis C – and apparently mine was the worst type. Hey ho, I thought, here we go again.

The doctors were adamant that I needed to get rid of the virus before I could even think about coming off methadone. They put me through a series of tests to measure my 'viral load'. It sounded really frightening and I wasn't much happier when they told me the results.

'It's going to be tough. We found a lot of the virus and frankly, the treatment is going to be Hell.'

No change there, then.

The first thing I had to do was to prove that I was completely clean of alcohol for three months. At my worst – or at least my recent worst – I'd been drinking one of those quarter bottles of vodka every day. Because Hepatitis

34

C attacks the liver – which is where all that booze ended up – the doctors wanted to be sure there wasn't a drop left in my body.

The treatment itself was going to take 28 weeks – just over half a year of constant injections and tests and more injections, and yet more tests. They told me that the effects of the drugs I'd be putting into my system were so strong that I wouldn't be up to doing anything for a few days after each injection. Put simply, I'd be laid out and barely able to move.

All of which meant that I had to find somewhere permanent to live. Eddie had been incredibly kind and supportive but there was no way I could put him through what was coming, even if I'd been able to manage it there. And then my luck turned: with the support of my social worker, the council found me a flat. And not just any flat, but a lovely little one-bedroom place in a good part of town and with wonderful views over the Northumberland hills. Mum went with me to look at it and the moment I saw it, two things flashed into my mind.

The first was that it felt like somewhere I could – at last – make a home. The second was: 'Who on earth would paint bedroom walls bright orange and the rest of the rooms in sea-blue, with a nauseous wave pattern on them?' Mum and I looked at each other and suddenly grinned; we had a job on!

It helped that Mum had just taken voluntary redundancy and so for the next three months – as my body got rid of any trace of alcohol – we got rid of any trace of orange and wavy-blue. When we'd finished, the little flat felt like home – and Mum and I were closer than we'd ever been in our lives. For the first time in years I actually began to see that I had a future.

But first there was the little business of Hepatitis C. As soon as I started the treatment, I realised that the doctor hadn't been exaggerating: it really was Hell. Every Monday for 28 weeks I had to inject myself with pegylated interferon – a synthetic version of a naturally occurring protein in everyone's body that stimulates the immune system to attack all the cells of the virus. The effects were almost immediate: I was knocked completely flat for the next three days with a flu-like fever.

But there were more gradual side effects, too. The most noticeable was that all my hair fell out. I've always had lots of naturally wavy auburn locks but within weeks of starting the treatment, I was completely bald. I also felt constantly sick – not just queasy, but hit by wave upon wave of deep-down nausea. My skin began to itch severely, but no matter how much I scratched it there was no relief.

And then the cruellest thing of all hit me: depression. This is a recognised side effect of the treatment, coupled with insomnia and sudden anxiety attacks. But to me the depression was far worse because I'd just begun to feel hope again. Now I was back at rock bottom. Again.

Those 28 weeks of injections followed by fevers, with a constant backdrop of feeling physically and mentally miserable, seemed to drag on for ever. Even my new home began to feel like a prison. Mum and I saw each other almost every day during the treatment and she did her best to lift my spirits. It must have been awful for her but somehow she stuck with it – and stuck by me, no matter how irritable or difficult I was. But eventually it ended. I went back for my final blood test and was given the news that filled my lungs with new air and my body with new strength: I was cured of Hepatitis C.

Now it was time for me to repay Mum. After the court case I'd made her a promise that I was going to get myself off methadone and with the hepatitis out of my system, I was determined to keep my word.

The most common way of trying to bring an addict off methadone is to reduce their dosage very, very gradually over a long period. Normally a clinic will start with an introductory 10 per cent reduction for the first two weeks and then carry on with a series of 5 per cent reductions over many months until the magic figure of 20 milligrams is reached. I was on 60 milligrams daily, which meant that my first reduction would only bring me down to 54 milligrams – and at the rate of 5 per cent every step down, it would take at least seven or eight months to get to 20 milligrams.

That figure has achieved an almost legendary status among addicts: put a bunch of people together on a methadone reduction programme and the biggest question everyone asks each other is how close they are to 20 milligrams. Why? It's the last big hurdle. Every doctor, scientist and junkie agrees that the last 20 milligrams is the hardest and frequently it takes even longer to get from there to zero than it has to get to 20 milligrams in the first place.

All in all, my target of 12 weeks seemed ridiculous. I was

in for a year – maybe longer – and that's assuming I could cope with the constant cravings that would result from an ever-reducing dose. But something inside me rebelled: I didn't want it to take 12 months. I'd said 12 weeks and I meant it. I wanted to be free of the monkey on my back – free to enjoy the hope of new life, to be a normal person with normal friends, not fellow addicts. Also, I wanted to repay Mum for everything she'd done for me. And so I ignored all the medical advice and set out to do it my way.

Was I mad? Certainly, every textbook tells you that the longer the reduction programme, the higher the chances of long-term abstinence. But I was Sarah Forsyth: I'd been through the Hell of Amsterdam and being forced to have sex with more than a dozen men a day, and I'd survived. I'd been a crack whore with a £500-a-day cocaine habit and I'd survived. I'd seen someone I knew and cared for shot in the head, just a few feet away from my drugged eyes, and I'd survived.[1] Was I going to let the sticky, sweet green liquid cosh defeat me? No bloody way!

But not even my determination could insulate me from the pain. From the first day that I embarked on my rapid reduction regime, it hit me: my body was in total shock. I ached all over – every bone felt like someone was tearing its heart out from the inside. There was no way I could manage food – the most I could cope with was a protein drink. And my mind was in constant over-drive. It was as if my brain had a life of its own: whatever I tried, it just wouldn't shut down, day or night. I was 'rattling'.

Every single day for almost four months I forced myself through this personal Hell. 24 hours a day, seven days a week. And then gradually, oh so gradually, I could see some light ahead. Being on methadone is like living – no, existing – in a thick fog. Everything around you is fuzzy and everything you try to do feels like wading through a thick swamp, with sucking water and thick tendrils of superhuman plants clinging to your body and slowing its progress to almost a standstill.

Now that fog began to lift. Not suddenly in the way that sunshine breaks through on a crisp autumn morning, but hazily staining through the soft, pillowy clouds that surrounded me.

And I wished it hadn't.

As the fog began to lift, the memories of all I'd been through began seeping back into my mind. The years of being sexually abused – first by my dad, then in the care home. I felt the painfully brief hope I'd had when I'd been offered the 'job' working with children in Amsterdam. With a terrible searing clarity, I witnessed again the moment a gun had been pointed at my head outside Schiphol airport and the vicious words of the man who had tricked me there echoed through my head: 'I'm going to show you where you'll be working, but it's not where you think: there's no crèche and you're not going to be a nursery nurse.'

I re-lived the first day when I was forced to have sex with my traffickers' clients, then the days and nights, forced to prostitute my drug-ravaged body in Amsterdam's Red Light District. All the faces of those selfish, thoughtless men who'd used me for their ugly pleasure passed in front of my eyes.

Once again I felt each callous brutality inflicted on me by the Yugoslavian pimps and criminals I was sold to. I heard the click of a pistol as it cocked and saw in slow motion the face of the poor, terrified Thai prostitute I had come to know as it exploded with the impact of the bullet.

Just as my body became used to functioning without the methadone, my mind grew tormented by the memories. Without the comforting numbness of the drug to blot everything out all the wounds were open and raw. I sobbed and wept, and curled into a ball with pain. Day and night, night and day.

And this is what everyone – all the politicians and policy makers in their nice clean offices with nice ordinary lives – forget. Most people don't take drugs for fun: they take them to hide from what they can't face or live with.

I hadn't voluntarily become an addict: I'd had addiction thrust upon me, though in a bitter twist of irony, without the drugs I probably wouldn't have survived Amsterdam and the endless stream of men satisfying their cruel lusts on and in my body. But the principle remains the same: drugs hid me from myself and all that had happened to me. Without them, I was truly alone.

Except that I wasn't. Not really – even though I struggled to see it sometimes.

Mum was with me every step of the way. Holding me, soothing me, drying my tears. Her strength, her faith (thank you again, Saint Monica) and her determination not to lose her daughter now that she'd come so far helped drag me through this latest Hell. Until one day, the fog was completely gone. The mental scars were still there (they always will be), but a clean, protective skin – thin and fragile, though it might be – had begun to heal over them. I had been in my new home for over six months.

I looked out of my window and saw that it was spring. There were buds on the trees and the distant hills were beginning to lose the coldness of the winter months. The air was fresh and for the first time in more than 20 years, I felt clean. It was the season of new life, and I felt it was time for my new life to begin.

There was just one thing I had to do first: I had to go back to Hell.

---

[1] Sarah was forced to watch a fellow sex slave murdered during the filming of a snuff porn tape in Amsterdam (see *Slave Girl*, John Blake Publishing Limited, 2009).

CHAPTER THREE

THE DECISION

**GANG WHO LURED SLOVAKIAN TEENAGER INTO SEX
SLAVERY IN BRITAIN JAILED FOR 52 YEARS.**

A gang of evil pimps and brothel keepers who lured
a teenage girl into a life of 'sexual slavery' in the
UK were jailed for a total of 52-and-a-half years
today. The 16-year-old virgin from Slovakia was
repeatedly raped and made to work in brothels in
Cambridgeshire, Bedfordshire and Middlesex. She
left her village with the promise of a legitimate job
in a pub but was imprisoned in a world of 'pimps,
brothels, prostitutes, traffickers and rapists',
Southwark Crown Court heard.

Daily Mail, 4 November 2008, London

Somewhere I had seen it. Somewhere in the flat – in a box still waiting to be unpacked or in a drawer – I still had it. I'd torn it from a newspaper. God knows where I'd come across it since the *Daily Mail* wasn't exactly my usual reading, if I'd even read a daily paper in those still-dark days. But I knew I'd seen it, and I knew I still had it.

What do you do when you come face-to-face with evil? What did *you* do when you read that story? Maybe across the breakfast table, maybe over a glass of wine at the end of a hard day's work. What did you do – what do any of us do?

I turned the flat upside down. Eventually I found it: torn from the paper and folded into an uneven square of newsprint, ragged at the edges and stained with heaven knows what. And I read it, quickly at first, then slowly over again.

Passed from one gang of people smugglers to another, the teenager was beaten, sexually assaulted and forced to take drugs at knifepoint.

During the six-week trial, prosecutor Jason Dunn-Shaw told the court: 'Slavery is alive and well and thrives in this country. The slaves are no longer Africans seized from the sun but young women from Eastern Europe. They are not brought in ships at gunpoint, but they are shackled nonetheless. Their shackles are not made of iron but consist of intimidation, threats of violence, actual violence and blackmail.'

But who were these sex slavers – men who traded and re-traded the body of a terrified teenager? Astonishingly – or so it seemed to me – they were part of a family business. Mesut Arslan was found guilty of one count of keeping a brothel used for prostitution – Arslan's brothel keeper uncle Ali Arslan was jailed for 14 years. His nephew, Mesut Arslan, 26, was locked up for two-and-a-half-years.

But there were others, too. Slovakian Edward Facuna, 54, who trafficked the teen, and his associate, Roman Pacan, 39, originally from the Czech Republic, were both jailed for 11 years. And then there was a Kosovan, 29-year-old Martin Doci, who trafficked the girl within the UK, and was found guilty of controlling a child prostitute along with the Arslans. He was locked up for 11 years. And finally, the gang's enforcer was an Albanian, Valmir Gjetja, also 29, who used violence to control the helpless teen, was jailed for three years. The more I read the more familiar the story sounded.

The girl's 16-month ordeal began when Facuna, a friend of her mother's, told her he could get her a job in a Peterborough pub. He and co-defendant Pacan drove the victim to Britain, but in Peterborough she was passed on to a man known only as 'Claude'.

Sobbing, she told the court: 'He started touching me all over my body. I said stop but he started more and more.'

The man, who was not before the court, then raped her. Within days he drove her to Ealing, west London, where she was made to work in a brothel.

Speaking in broken English the girl said: 'He buy me clothes like mini-skirt, bras and knickers with Playboy on them and he buy short tops. He buy me make-up and I was thinking it is cold, why is he buying me these clothes?'

Her questions were soon answered when 'Claude', who also confiscated the girl's ID card, dropped her at a flat above a coffee shop, where she was forced to have sex with four men on her first night. Describing the bordello she said: 'There was some kind of beating things, and handcuffs on the table and pictures of naked people. There was a double bed in the room.'

After a few weeks, she was 'bought' by Doci, who introduced her to the Arslans, proprietors of the Mellows Sauna in Bedford Road, Luton.

She began to work as a prostitute at the sauna after a few days in the hope she would be able to send money home to her mother.

'After a few days I said OK. I didn't have anybody and if I run away from that place then I have nobody.' Ali Arslan later bought the girl from Doci for £2,500. Finally she was handed to Gjetja, whom she initially believed would free her from the cycle of sex and violence.

She lived with him and his girlfriend at Avon Road, in Greenford, west London, for nearly seven months until she managed to run away when he attacked her with a knife after she refused to join him in snorting cocaine.

Jurors were told the brothel only served Turkish punters, who would pay between £60 for 20 minutes and £120 for an hour with the girls. The cash she earned was then divided between her Albanian 'owner' and Ali Arslan.

Sentencing Judge Martin Beddoe said: 'The principal activities with which this case has been concerned, in particular in respect of the first four defendants, are despicable and cannot be tolerated in a civilised society.

'In opening the case, the Crown told the jury that slavery is alive and well and this is what this case has essentially been about. Each of you in your various ways is playing a role in a degrading activity that produces untold misery amongst trafficked women. It exploits the impoverished, the young and the socially disadvantaged.

'Those exploited in such a way by false promises are entitled and deserve the protection of the law and those who engage in their exploitation whether it is traffickers or those who end up exploiting the trafficked must be dealt with and will be dealt with.'

As I read the report, I began weeping. Everything that poor, terrified young girl went through had happened to me but my ordeal had happened 12 years before and in a foreign country. This was 2008, this was England – surely it couldn't still be happening? Surely it couldn't be happening here?

And then I read the words again. Ealing. Luton. Ordinary little places – dull, even. Not some anonymous, squalid run-down city.

People live there; they get up, make their kids breakfast, pack them off to school and head out to work. They come home; they eat supper, do homework, go to the pub or watch TV. Could they really be the same places where a panic-stricken teenager from halfway across Europe was lured with false hopes, then raped and forced into sexual slavery? Why didn't someone stop it?

Stop right there and read that last sentence again. Why didn't someone stop it? Now try and answer the question. Maybe you've got an answer. Whatever it is, it's going to be the wrong one because the person who didn't stop it is *you*. It's all of us who live in our so-called civilised, educated country and yet somehow turn a blind eye to slavery, even when it happens in plain sight in commercial businesses on the streets of our towns and cities.

The newspaper cutting stirred something inside me. I saw clearly that this 21st-century slavery happened because we allowed it to take place. And we can't say we didn't know about it because we did: it was reported in our daily papers. Something must be done.

The more I thought about it, the more I wanted to know. Was this an isolated case or part of something much more common? Who was this young girl who had gone through everything I had? Were there more like her and if so, where did they come from? And above all else, who was supposed to stop this from happening?

Over the next few days an idea took shape in my mind. It seemed to me that I was as much to blame as everyone else, probably more so. After all, most people who read that story just dismissed it from their minds, considering it to have no relevance to their daily lives. But I was different. Not only had I been a sex slave just like that young Slovakian girl, but after I'd escaped and while in the depths of my addictions, I'd briefly – to my eternal shame – helped run a brothel.[1] If I didn't stand up and be counted, how could I blame anyone else for turning a blind eye?

I talked it over with Mum. Now that I was clean of drink and drugs, and my life was back on a normal track, I wanted – no, I *needed* – to put all those terrible experiences to some good use, I told her. I had decided to investigate sex trafficking and sex slavery; I had decided to go back to Hell.

Not unreasonably, Mum's reaction was to worry. After 15 terrible years, she'd only just got her daughter back and now here I was, proposing to re-immerse myself in the whole sordid and violent netherworld from which I'd fought so hard to escape. Was this really a good idea? Would I be strong enough to cope? And would I be putting myself in danger again?

We talked and talked for days. As we went back and forth over the whole thing, I remembered another conversation we'd had just before I set off for Amsterdam. Mum had been adamant that it was a bad idea and that I had no idea of the risks I was taking. I'd been full of breezy self-confidence and had ignored her fears. That time she'd been proved right – God, had she ever! Was I about to repeat the same mistake? Somehow this felt different: something inside me kept burning away – how could I not take this on? If the past 15 years were to mean anything, if they were not to be completely wasted, surely I needed to turn them to a positive purpose?

With Mum's support, I made the decision to go back into the Hell of sex trafficking. It was a journey that would take all the newfound strength I had – and all the love of those around me. If I'd known from the outset how painful the journey would be, I honestly don't know if I would have set out on it. But in that moment I knew that, finally, I had a very real purpose in my life: I was going on a journey to find the slaves I had left behind.

---

[1] See *Slave Girl*, John Blake Publishing Limited, 2009.

CHAPTER FOUR

THE ELEPHANT AND THE BLIND MEN

Like most children I loved stories.

As well as traditional fairy stories, some of my favourites were old fables – the sort you used to get in Ladybird books or big volumes, like *Aesop's Fables*. One of them in particular has always stuck with me. Let me tell it to you.

Once upon a long time ago, there was an emperor who ruled a land with the help of a number of very wise men. One day he decided to see just how wise they were. He told all the wise men to put on blindfolds so that they couldn't see anything, then he had his servants bring an elephant into the room.

He instructed each of the wise men to feel a different part of the elephant and then to identify exactly what the object was. The one who felt a leg said it was a pillar; the one who felt the tail said it was a rope; the one who felt the trunk insisted it was the branch of a tree, while the one who felt the head claimed it was a pot. And so it went on: the wise man who felt the elephant's belly said the object was a wall; and the one who felt its tusk was certain it was a solid pipe.

None of the wise men could agree with any of the others and soon they fell to quarrelling and fighting. Then the emperor told them to stop their arguing and to listen to each other so they could put together all of the parts they'd touched: when they did so, the wise men suddenly realised that it was an elephant.

The fable is supposed to teach us that no one has the whole truth about anything and only when we put together the entire picture can we understand what it is we are really up against. It's a pretty little story and one that's been around for hundreds of years in all different cultures across the world. The sad thing about it is that we don't learn the lesson.

The fable of the *Elephant and The Blind Men* popped into my head very quickly as I began my journey back into sex slavery. There was a vast amount of information readily available but it was all in pieces and no one seemed to be putting it all together to show the whole picture. There were lots of tusks, trunks, heads and bodies, but no overall elephant.

The first thing I wanted to know was how many prostitutes there are in Britain today. If I was to find out how many of them had been tricked and trafficked like me, then I needed to start with the actual number of women (and it is mostly women) in the sex trade. But no one knows. There are estimates, of course: most of them reckon that on any given day there are around 100,000 people working in prostitution. But really these are more 'guesstimates' than estimates. They're pulled together from various individual local studies and the total figure is arrived at by a rough-and-ready bit of maths.

That was my first big shock. I know from personal experience how vulnerable prostitutes are to violence, intimidation and drugs, let alone being owned and controlled by sex slavers. How could we not have discovered how many women like me there are? And how could we, now well into the 21st century, still be so complacent?

Perhaps not surprisingly, the only real attempt I could find to do any large-scale research was by a women's charity dedicated to helping the victims of sex trafficking. The Poppy Project (which can be found on the website www.eavesforwomen.org.uk) has done some amazing work and I truly wish there had been something like Poppy in Amsterdam when I was there. It has helped hundreds of women, providing them with a physical refuge from their traffickers and the emotional or psychological support many of them need to deal with the horrific scars of being enslaved in the sex industry.

Researchers for the Poppy Project set out to discover how many brothels were operating in London – and also to find out as much as they could about where the women who worked in them came from and how they'd got there. All the brothels they targeted advertised in newspapers across the city. They started with a list of 1,500 brothels (though many called themselves 'saunas' or advertised 'massage'). The researchers made contact with 921 of them. London has 33 separate boroughs: the Poppy Project found an average of 28 brothels in each and every borough. Westminster – one of the wealthiest parts of London and the home of Parliament and Scotland Yard – had 71. And where were these brothels? Mostly in residential neighbourhoods – the sorts of places with families and children: three quarters of all the 'massage parlours' and 'saunas' were on the high street. People walked past them (and obviously some walked into them) every day, in broad daylight, and no one seemed to worry.

To me it was shocking: behind the doors of ordinary houses and in commercial shop premises men were calmly walking in and buying sex from women. This wasn't Amsterdam; it wasn't a Red Light District, where organised prostitution was legal – this was part of the very fabric of our day-to-day lives. And the number of women was huge: the researchers identified at least 1,933 individual prostitutes working in London brothels. On average they were 21 years old.

Who were the women behind these doors and shop fronts? Where did they come from? And was anyone actually checking to find out if they were there willingly? That was the next shock. And the one after that, too.

The Poppy Project's investigation found the women were from 77 – that's 77 – different nationalities and ethnic backgrounds. Some – a very few – were British, of course, but nearly half came from Eastern Europe; another third came from Thailand, China and other Asian countries. And there were women from Ghana, Nigeria and South America. How could a young girl from Ghana – let alone China – end up working in a brothel in Britain? Did she travel here by herself or did someone pay for her passage? I had a nasty feeling: I'd been their age when I ended up a prisoner in Amsterdam's sex market. I couldn't have deliberately found my way into the Red Light District, much less set about selling my body in a country whose language, laws and customs I didn't understand. How much more difficult would it have been for these young women to decide to come halfway across the world to set themselves up as prostitutes in London? And why would they pick Britain?

But there were no answers to those questions. The Poppy Project had done its research by having male investigators pose as customers and ask the brothel owners for information. None of them was going to admit trafficking in sex slaves.

As if that wasn't bad enough, what happened next was a classic case of *The Elephant and The Blind Men*. Other organisations – university academics, rival research groups and campaigners for legalised prostitution – immediately attacked the Poppy Project's investigation for not being sufficiently scientific. Quite how much science you need to ring up brazenly advertising brothels and ask what's on offer is beyond me: what I do know is that the whole issue got caught up in the tangled weeds of Wise Men arguing – and the women in the brothels were forgotten.

It was the same story wherever I looked: individual bits of research, with little snapshots of the situation in towns and cities across the UK. And what was most depressing was that everyone seemed to deal mostly in statistics. These were women – young women mostly – in a dangerous and underground industry, but no one seemed to ask about their stories; no one seemed to want to find out how they had got here or whether they were willingly selling themselves to men.

Could I do any better? I wanted to, that's for sure. Just the chance that one of these women had been trafficked and forced into prostitution like me was enough and on the surface it seemed there were a lot more than just one woman. But what could I do? How could Sarah Forsyth from Gateshead, with no relevant qualifications and still recovering from the effects of sex slavery herself, do better than all these clever academics and trained researchers?

She could start by looking – really looking – that's how. Not at one bit of the elephant but at the whole damn beast. It might not be scientific but I was determined that I wouldn't let these women down.

But the sheer size of this particular elephant was daunting. Just by checking the adverts in my local newspapers I discovered that there were more than 40 brothels operating – advertising – in the Newcastle and Gateshead areas alone. On top of that there were escort agencies (which apparently don't count as brothels, even though they openly boast about having dozens and dozens of prostitutes who will come to homes and hotels to sell sex). There was no chance I could go to each of these sex markets and start asking questions about the women they were selling, but there was another way.

He calls himself 'Galahad'. It's a bit of an ironic name, really: the original 'Sir Galahad' was one of King Arthur's Knights of the Round Table. He's immortalised in children's storybooks for his honour, purity and gallantry.

The 'Galahad' I was after was the very opposite to everything the romantic myths of Camelot stood for, though he's just as difficult to track down. He's a British man who emigrated to the Midwest of the United States but set up an Internet business in California advertising brothels in Britain. 'PunterNet' has been online for more than a decade and one of its main 'attractions' is a message board, where men post reviews of the prostitutes they have visited. And they do: there are thousands upon thousands of what PunterNet calls 'Field Reports', listed in alphabetical order by town, date and 'author'.

It's a horrible and dispiriting site without any shame (though with the anonymity of the Internet). Men describe exactly what they were able to do to the woman whose body they used and give ratings for how well she performed. Scrolling through them, I began to feel sick.

What made it worse was that 'Galahad' likes to pose as someone who helps fight sex trafficking. He instructs his 'punters' to report any sign that a prostitute is being forced to work against her will and lists the phone number for Crimestoppers. And he's convinced that they would. In a statement posted on the website he wrote:

> The people who use this site (and the many others like it) are decent folk and would not hesitate to make that call to Crimestoppers if they suspected something was

not right. So, sites like PunterNet are helping to REDUCE trafficking and slavery, which is what the Government claims to want to accomplish.

There isn't, of course, a single shred of evidence that any of them have done that, which is probably why in September 2009 the (then) Deputy Prime Minister, Harriet Harman, demanded the Governor of California Arnold Schwarzenegger close down the PunterNet website.

'It is truly degrading and puts women at risk,' she said. 'PunterNet has pages and pages of women for sale in London. But PunterNet is based in California so I've raised it with the US Ambassador to London and I've called on California's governor Arnie Schwarzenegger. Surely it can't be too difficult for the Terminator to terminate PunterNet and that's what I am demanding that he does.'

But maybe it was, for Arnie didn't do anything. The American Ambassador to London politely explained that PunterNet was protected by the US Constitution and its guaranteed right of free speech. In fact, the only real effect was to increase the number of people who logged on to the website. 'Galahad' boasted that on the very day Harriet Harman made her impassioned speech on behalf of women in prostitution PunterNet received 2.7 million hits – more than double the normal daily traffic.

And I was one of them.

I've always believed in turning the weapons used against you back on those who hold them. Even during my worst moments in Amsterdam I tried to think of ways to turn the tables on the men who abused my broken body. Now

PunterNet would be my Trojan Horse, my way into organised brothels with the men who bought sex being my eyes and ears.

I began by working through the 'Field Reports'. There was barely a town without at least half a dozen 'reviews' of women working in prostitution. Every city had dozens, sometimes hundreds, of reports. Villages, too – small, rural communities you would think couldn't have a brothel – but they do. Lots of them.

As I read through page after awful page of men unashamedly describing what they had done, I wondered what they would have said about me. Would they have written – as many did – that I was a 'real girlfriend experience'? Or, like so many of the reviews, that I was dead-eyed, uninterested in them and desperate to get the whole sordid, painful business over with?

Because that's the first thing that struck me. For every glowing account of a wonderfully willing and enthusiastic sexual encounter there were just as many in which the men saw how much the woman hated it. They saw it, they thought about it – and then they wrote a review, not saying how badly they felt, but how badly they felt *cheated*. I wanted to scream at them: 'What the hell did you expect? Why can't you wake up to what you're doing? That woman you have just dismissed with careless and callous phrase was trying to communicate – as best she could – that she wasn't doing this willingly.'

Would they have listened if somehow my silent voice could have reached them? Maybe, but I doubt it. Would they – as 'Galahad' so confidently boasted – have picked up the phone and called Crimestoppers? Do me a favour: don't insult my intelligence.

This led me to the next thing I noticed. Review after review revealed a little bit more about where these women came from. Here's a typical one – from Gateshead, my home town, and no more than half a mile from my little flat.

Girl's Name: Petra.
Location: Nice house on quiet (and quite decent-looking) estate. Good free car parking, not many people about, but slightly concerned people in the area knew what was going on, etc.
Description: Exactly as described – tall, slim blonde, firm skin, very pretty girl. Of Eastern European decent (possibly Russian?).
Score: Overall I would rate my visit as 7.5/10.
Comments: The GFE [Girl Friend Experience] is what lets the score down slightly (not too much though). Petra doesn't kiss on the mouth but the main thing for me was that she didn't engage in any eye contact during sex – she looked away the whole time, which was slightly disappointing. She made noises throughout, like um argh, but in translation it seemed a bit put on (sure it probably was!).

Do something for me. Read all of that again. Slowly. Notice anything?

'Petra' is Russian or Eastern European. She didn't engage in eye contact. She looked away while this 'reviewer' was using her body and 'put on' noises to encourage him – but in a language that wasn't her own. Now, do you think this 'punter' called Crimestoppers? Do you think he ever once considered that she might not be in that 'nice house on a decent-looking estate' of her own free will? That she might – just might – have been trafficked there? You tell me. No, better yet: you tell 'Galahad'.

A glimpse into the possible truth about PunterNet and the brothels it advertises came a few months after I'd started my journey into the sex trafficking industry today. Just before Christmas 2009, Norfolk Police raided a series of interlinked brothels in Norwich, Great Yarmouth, King's Lynn and Ipswich. All had been advertised with reviews on PunterNet.

When the police broke down the doors they found British men in the act of having sex with semi-naked Chinese and Thai women. One of them was Mai Ling, a postgraduate student of Bangkok University. As a child she'd dreamed of becoming a vet and had been smuggled to England with the promise of a good job. She knew it wouldn't be legal – she had no right to work in Britain – but felt she had no choice because her family needed the money to pay for her father's liver transplant.

What her traffickers never told her – until she arrived – was that she 'owed' them another £24,000; nor that she would have to work as a prostitute to pay off this 'debt'. She was forced to have sex with four men every night for many months and told the police she was 'scared'.

Did any of those men call Crimestoppers to report that they'd abused a terrified young woman who couldn't speak

English, let alone have arranged, all by herself, willingly to work in a Norwich brothel? You tell me.

And there was another telling part of the story. Mai Ling's owner – for that's what it amounted to – was Yi Yuan Geng, a Chinese woman living in London. Police discovered she ran up to six brothels across the region, filling them with women from Southeast Asia who had been trafficked and forced to pay off 'debts' by servicing the brothels' clients. Geng was sentenced to 18 months in prison, to be followed by deportation.

But how was she allowed to set up in the sex business in the first place? Chinese nationals have no legal right to live and work here, much less set up a string of brothels. The more I looked into British sex slavery, the more cases I found of foreign criminals trafficking women into prostitution throughout the British Isles. So, did it make me angry? You bet it did.

Don't get me wrong here. It's not the fact that these sex slavers weren't British that annoyed me: I have contempt for anyone – whatever their nationality – who makes money from the sexual abuse of vulnerable women. That includes me, as it happens, and I hate myself for it.

The point that struck me, though, is that foreign criminals running illegal brothels here should stand out just that little bit more than some thoughtless, selfish British sex slaver – especially when they bring in their cargo of flesh from the other side of the world. Shouldn't that trigger some red flag somewhere? Wasn't anyone paying attention?

The answer, it appears, is sometimes; only sometimes.

Everywhere I looked, there were cases of sex traffickers being prosecuted. And every time someone said: 'These are just the tip of the iceberg.' If that's true then it must be a *Titanic*-size iceberg, because the cases that went to court – the cases we know about – are horrific.

Take Carl Pritchett. When I began my journey back into sex slavery in 2009, Pritchett had made a fortune from it. The owner of Cuddles 'massage parlour' on Birmingham's Hagley Road, he drove a Ferrari and had bought himself a string of houses, both at home and abroad. And not surprisingly, the brothel had an average of 490 'clients' a week, bringing Pritchett £3.5 million in profit. When West Midland Police raided Cuddles they found 19 women inside 'servicing' those clients. And where had these women come from?

Two years in prison – just two years – for running a brothel; two years for a millionaire's lifestyle built on sex slavery. Does that seem right to you?

And it got worse. The court that convicted Pritchett ordered him to hand over £2 million of his profits. When he refused, another court sent him back to prison. But this time the sentence was seven years. Apparently failing to hand over your ill-gotten gains is three times more serious than having 19 women from 10 different countries in your shabby and sordid 'massage parlour'.

Maybe you think that's right. Maybe you think (though I hope you don't) that in some way this was a 'victimless crime'; that's certainly what the men who were caught taking their selfish pleasure with these poor young women thought (at least those who didn't pull up their trousers and run away): they claimed they were doing nothing wrong. I see it differently; I know this isn't a victimless crime. And I've been in the victim's (stiletto) shoes.

Because however you dress it up, however you dress us up, we're no more than pieces of meat to these men. At least to the sex traffickers we have a value (not that we ever see anything of it). Exactly what sort of value was dramatically revealed just before Christmas 2009. The Metropolitan Police released a picture that was shocking for its appalling banality – and for the sheer brazen confidence of a group of Albanian sex traffickers.

Oxford Street is London's busiest shopping street. Nearly 200 million tourists walk up and down it every year, spending almost £6 billion. With all those shops and all those people, it's no surprise that the street is full of security cameras; everyone knows they're there. And yet it was in the middle of Oxford Street, in front of crowds of shoppers and under the gaze of security cameras that two Albanian men sold a shivering 20-year-old Lithuanian girl to a brothel owner. And the price? £3,000. CCTV cameras captured the entire deal on videotape. The pictures clearly show the brothel owner calmly handing over a wad of notes to the Albanians, while people walk calmly by.

Luckily for the girl, police were watching and moved in to rescue her. According to the detectives, had they not done so the Lithuanian girl would have been taken to a brothel in East London and made to earn her new owner £100,000 a year by having sex up to 25 times a day. How did they know? Because they'd just raided another brothel owned by the same gang. Inside that one they found a 16-

year-old girl, also from Lithuania. She told the officers who freed her that she had believed she was coming to London for a romantic weekend with her boyfriend, but he had instead handed her over to a gang of pimps.

Remember that research by the Poppy Project? The one that discovered there are nearly 2,000 prostitutes working in London? Do you know how many of them are from foreign countries? Almost 97 per cent of them.

Did they come here of their own free will, travelling thousands of miles – past the legal Red Light Districts of Germany and Holland – to work in grubby illegal East End brothels in London? Or did someone trick and traffic them here, then force them to have sex with hundreds of men every single week? What do you think?

Another town, but the same story: Sheffield this time. An old northern city which fell on hard times when the steel industry which had supported it largely closed down, yet also a city which prides itself on its modern and forward-looking regeneration schemes – and its determination to bring new foreign investment and jobs into the area.

Josef Demeter and Natasa Demeterova arrived in Sheffield in 2005. Within three years they had, in their own way, brought in foreign money and jobs. They set up a scheme offering local employment to young women from Slovakia and the Czech Republic, none of whom spoke English, and at least one was homeless and destitute. But there were no 'jobs' and when they got to Sheffield, the women were told they had to work as prostitutes in two brothels owned by the Demeters.

I know what you're thinking: how could they force these women to do something they didn't want to do? Surely they could have got away? That's the same thing that was always said to me: why didn't you escape? And the answer is always the same: fear.

When the Demeters were eventually caught and prosecuted, one of the victims – who was only 17 when she arrived – gave her evidence via videolink. She told the court that she tried to say no, but that Demeterova began:

Shouting hysterically, I could not stop doing it because I was afraid of them.

Demeterova got six years in jail for her part in the trafficking and sexual exploitation of the women. Josef Demeter did a runner abroad and had to be extradited back to Britain to face trial. He was jailed for four years and nine months after finally admitting people trafficking for sexual exploitation. While sentencing them, Judge John Swanson said: 'These girls were all in their own ways vulnerable – none of them spoke any English, none of them had any money. Their means of communication or even travelling within this country after their introduction would have been extremely limited.

'I am also quite clear in my mind that you were to an extent able to bully them into working harder as prostitutes and that you and your husband were both responsible for attaining as much money from them as you could extract.

'These are serious offences because they prey on human weakness and also upon human misery.'

And Detective Sergeant Alisdair Duncan, one of the police officers involved in the raid on the couple's brothels, gave a statement to the local press, saying: 'We talk about 200 years since the abolition of slavery, but this is a new kind of slavery where women are forced to work in the sex trade.'

I don't disagree with a word of that but there is a phrase, a really important phrase, that's missing – 'blind eye'. What everyone involved in the case seemed to ignore was how Josef Demeter and Natasa Demeterova were caught. South Yorkshire Police only mounted a raid after one of the desperate girls managed to escape and telephone her home in Slovakia, telling her mother she had been forced into the sex trade and didn't know where she was.

If she hadn't done so then no one – not the police, not the local council (which would have collected business taxes from the 'massage parlours'), not the clients who took advantage of the scared and enslaved women within them – would have lifted a finger to close down the sex slavery carried out in full view on the streets of Sheffield.

There's one other really important word in that story: fear.

The women – girls, really – the Demeters trafficked were terrified of them. And it's the same story wherever you look, just as it was for me. Everywhere – and I mean everywhere – I came across case after case of women being tricked and trafficked into the most callous and brutal sex slavery imaginable, and kept there by fear.

In rural Wales, a family of sex slavers were discovered to be running a multi-million pound prostitution business from an old vicarage. Their victims – some as young as 14 – were shipped from Nigeria to 35 brothels across Ulster and the Republic of Ireland. All of the women they trafficked were vulnerable; all came from poor family backgrounds and had lost one or both of their parents.

And how did these impoverished Nigerian girls – children some of them – end up in brothels half a world away? Their traffickers tricked them, that's how. They promised them jobs and a better life away from their remote rural villages. One was told she could be a hairdresser, another that she would be put into further education. Instead, they were issued with forged passports in different names and shipped to Dublin, and from there into a new 'life' of sex slavery.

According to Britain's Serious and Organised Crime Agency, which ran the investigation: 'The first sign these girls know they are going into a life of prostitution is when they are bought items of clothing, dropped off at a flat, and get a phone call to say 'expect a male customer and do what you are told.'

Just like me, these poor bewildered girls were forced to let men abuse their bodies for 12 to 15 hours a day and they were regularly moved from one brothel to another, making them even more isolated and vulnerable. Their owners – for that's what we're talking about, owners of other human beings – supplied them with 'necessities' – condoms, and lingerie. But the money they earned – the going rate was €160 for half an hour – was paid into the brothel owners' bank accounts.

So, who were these slave-owners? And how did they

manage to run such a business, importing young women from Africa to satisfy the lust of men across Ireland? It turned out that behind this new slave trade was a single family: Thomas Carroll, 48, an Irishman, and Shamiela Clark, 32, his South African wife – together with Carroll's 26-year-old daughter, Toma.

Can you imagine that? Could you run a business built on the backs of abused and terrified young Nigerian women? And do so with your own daughter?

What was even worse was the way the Carrolls' victims were prevented from escaping. When the family was eventually convicted in 2010 the court was told that many of the trafficked women and girls lived in fear of 'juju oaths' made during 'terrifying and humiliating' rituals they were forced into by their traffickers.

One was forced to sleep in a coffin to 'put the fear of death' in her. When she had her period, her blood was taken and put into a padlock; this was then locked, and thrown in the river. As far as the girl was concerned, this meant her life was no longer her own to control: she believed it was now in the hands of the River Goddess.

Reading this, maybe you're thinking that it sounds crazy – literally unbelievable. And to our modern Western eyes, maybe it does: we no longer live in fear of such superstitions. But to a young and defenceless girl from an isolated village in the middle of Nigeria, it was very real indeed.

Nor was the 'River Goddess' the only way the traffickers instilled fear. Live chickens were killed and the victims made to eat the raw hearts. They clipped off the girls' fingernails and pubic hair, keeping the clippings to 'instil the fear of God in them' and to show they could 'metaphysically' be reached wherever they were. Throughout these ceremonies the girls were kept naked, and one was cut all over her body with sharp blades.

And as if that wasn't bad enough, once they arrived in Ireland all the women were told that they had to pay back, on average, £65,000 to their traffickers. If they didn't – or couldn't – they (or their families back in Nigeria) would die.

The Carrolls' family business made them millions – enough to buy properties in South Africa, Bulgaria and Mozambique. And many other companies profited: when they raided the old vicarage, police found 70 mobile phones, all linked to adverts placed on sexual services websites or in newspapers. Over a period of just three months, the Carrolls spent £5,200 on one telephone bill: the invoice alone was 5,000 pages long.

Did those mobile phone companies know what they were being paid for? Did they ever bother to ask? Or did they – as everyone does – just turn a blind eye?

And what about the newspapers that carried the advert? In just one year the Carrolls spent £28,580 on newspaper advertising. £28,580: that's an awful lot of adverts. You'd think someone working on the newspapers might have noticed something, especially after reading the text. Here's a typical example:

African Nandi, very petite tanned chocolate delight, petite slim size 8, 34C but leggy flexible kinky, Nandi enjoys nudism and exploring her body and yours, making the sessions fun and intimate.

Did no one stop to think before accepting these adverts? Or did they simply put the money in the tills and carry on regardless. What do you think?

And that continual, convenient 'blindness' even made it into the courtroom. Cardiff Crown Court jailed Thomas Carroll for seven years and his wife got three and a half years, after both admitted conspiracy to control prostitution for gain and a further charge of money-laundering. Carroll's daughter was given a two-year prison sentence after admitting to laundering the profits of the family business – which, in one year alone, totalled more than £800,000. But during the sentencing Judge Neil Bidder made it clear he didn't blame the Carrolls for the way their victims came to be entrapped in their brothels. He told them: 'I'm not sentencing you for trafficking those women and accept you were unaware of the personal circumstance of the women who worked in your brothels and you were not responsible for any violence and threats of violence. But the Nigerian women who were threatened with dreadful coercion all ended up working for you.

'You did not ask and did not care what personal tragedies had befallen those women submitting for your profit.'

Isn't that like telling an 18th-century American slave-owner that he wasn't responsible for bringing African men, women and children to work on his lands? Of course he was responsible, just as the Carrolls were. If they – and people like them – didn't create a demand for Nigerian sex slaves, do you think anyone would be trafficking them?

The problem is that no one really listens to the women who are trafficked into sex slavery. God knows no one ever listened to me when I was trapped behind my pane of glass in Amsterdam's neon-lit windows. And no one really tells their stories: maybe it's because the women are ashamed of what has happened to them, as I certainly was. Or maybe it's just that what they – I – have to say is too painful to hear.

Will you hear it? Are you strong enough?

Openshaw is a grim, post-industrial mess of a suburb of Manchester; it makes even Gateshead look glamorous. At the same time as the South Yorkshire Police were prosecuting Josef Demeter and Natasa Demeterova in Sheffield and the Carrolls were about to face trial in Cardiff, a girl called Marinela Badea was enduring her third year of sex slavery in an Openshaw 'sauna' with the bitterly ironic name of 'Shangri-La'.

When I came across Marinela's story I wanted to weep and shout with anger, all at the same time. The fury was because everyone knows this happens every day, everywhere; the tears were because for the first time someone bothered to find out about the girl locked up in the brothel – even if they treated her like dirt at first.

Manchester Police had known about Shangri-La for years. They knew that it was a brothel and that the man who owned it, David Greenwood, had two more 'massage parlours' in the City. But the only interest the police showed in the businesses was to pop in occasionally and see if their owner had any tips on armed robbers and sex traffickers.

Stop right there: would you ask a brothel owner for tips about sex trafficking? Would you? But, more to the point, would you expect him to tell you the truth?

David Greenwood had owned the brothels for three years. He inherited them from his father. Each was filled with young women, many from Eastern Europe. Marinela was one of them. Her story came out in court – and it's a story that I knew only too well.

She had been trafficked from Romania when she was just 17, a schoolgirl in the provincial town of Alexandria, two hours' drive from Bucharest, Romania's capital. One day, in March 2008, she disappeared.

She had left school that day with a friend and gone to the flat they shared so they could both do their homework together. There was knock on the door: when Marinela opened it there were two men outside. One was a local man with an unsavoury reputation, the other one was a stranger: his name was Marius Nejloveanu.

The men invited Marinela and her friend to a barbecue. Marinela refused, telling them she needed to finish her homework. But the men weren't interested: they grabbed her, banged her head on a wardrobe and instructed her to put on her coat.

Then Marius saw my ID card on the table near the TV and took it and my phone. I asked him: 'Why are you taking my passport?' and he just stared at me.

Within just a couple of hours Marinela was raped and prostituted to a friend of Nejloveanu.

> I said: 'I want to go home', so they beat me up. After half an hour, they brought his friend in and they forced me to sleep with him. From that day they kept me prisoner. They wouldn't even let me go outside in case somebody saw me.

Throughout the first days of her captivity, Marinela's friends and family searched for the missing girl. No one could understand what had happened to her: she was devoted to her family and a diligent student at school. But the search never stood a chance for Marinela's abductors had already erased all legal trace of her. They had obtained a fake passport with a false name, changing her from a 17-year-old schoolgirl into a 21-year-old adult. Armed with this, they put her in the back of a car, drove to Bucharest, and forced her on to the 4am coach to England.

Two days later – on 3 April 2008 – Marinela arrived at the central bus station in Birmingham. Terrified and traumatised, she was in a foreign country with no idea what was happening: the last thing Nejloveanu told her was that she would be made to work for him in a 'cleaning job'.

A woman claiming to be a friend of Nejloveanu met her off the coach and drove her to a large house in Edgbaston, one of Birmingham's leafy, middle-class suburbs. She discovered that two other Romanian girls lived there. But any relief she felt at being with people who spoke her language was abruptly shattered.

One of them asked me: 'Do you know how to put a condom on?' I said: 'What are you talking about?' That's when it dawned on me.

The women told her she would be working in a nearby local brothel and told her to come with them. When she refused, they told her bluntly that unless she co-operated, Nejloveanu would kill her the moment he returned from Romania.

It was at this point in Marinela's story that I broke down and began to cry. I had been through exactly the same experience when I was trafficked to Holland. The girl I was with there – Sally, as I called her in my last book – had warned that if I didn't work as a prostitute then the man who had tricked and brought me there would kill me. I relived every moment of my first day in captivity as I sat through Marinela's testimony. With visceral, awful certainty, I knew exactly what her mind – and her body – had been going through.

Because whatever the mind does to try and block out the pain, the body reacts. Just like me, Marinela had stopped eating. And just like me, she began to waste away. She had been tiny before her abduction but now she could see her ribs stick out every time she breathed.

When Nejloveanu eventually arrived at the house Marinela was still refusing to be a prostitute. The result was even worse than the other girls had warned her.

He beat me up and forced me to sleep with him — anal sex. It really hurt. He was pulling my hair and hurting my back.

Sometimes he would bang my head right on the corner of the door. That really hurt.

She was brave – oh, how much braver than me – but in the end she had to give in and do as Nejloveanu told her. He had handed her a cheap and gaudy bra and pants – just as my trafficker had thrust some grubby 'sexy' lingerie at me – and driven to the brothel. Almost inevitably, it called itself 'a sauna'.

She was trapped there. Unable to speak a word of English, she had no way to say 'no' to her first client, even though she desperately wanted to tell him that she was doing this against her will, that she'd been kidnapped and trafficked. But she couldn't: all she could do was cry and hope that he would notice her pain and stop. He didn't, of course he didn't – but neither did any of the selfish, greedy men who abused her that same day and in the days afterwards. After all, who would care about a prostitute?

That first day she was raped often enough to 'earn' £300. The same amount of money would have supported her entire family back home in Romania for more than six weeks but such a calculation was irrelevant for she was forced to hand over every penny. And then to work harder.

After that I was making £400, £500. After a month I was making £500 a day, but if I wanted a cigarette or bar of chocolate I had to ask.

Every day she was forced to work in the brothel for 12 hours. Seven days a week, from 10am to 10pm. How many men used her in that period? An average of between 10 and 12 men a day. A minimum of 70 men a week. Did any of them have any qualms about paying £40 to abuse this young, stick-thin girl who cried and couldn't speak English? And did any of them do, as 'Galahad' and his PunterNet admirers say they would, and report her ordeal to Crimestoppers? Now what do you think?

Nejloveanu took half of each £40 'fee'. The brothel keeper took the other £20. And the men kept on coming. Most were white, a few of Asian origin. Some came back more than once, but mostly they were strangers. Often they would be drunk; sometimes they were violent.

> There was one guy and I didn't want to do what he asked me. So he beat me up because he was drunk, pulled my hair and slapped me. But they [the brothel management] just take the violent men outside. Nothing ever happens to them even if I am really hurt.

And she was never – ever – allowed to refuse to be pawed and penetrated by the brothel's customers.

> Even if they stink, and have come straight from work, you have to sleep with them – it was so horrible. Can you imagine how I was feeling, taking my clothes off, exposing the horrible underwear that Marius had bought? I was supposed to be in high school, not in England sleeping with men and making money for criminals.

Marinela's bruised and emaciated body was a cash machine – no more and no less, and a cash machine that would never be allowed to stop spewing out its profits.

Nejloveanu gave strict instructions that she was never to be allowed to step outside of the brothel. She once tried to escape but was quickly caught and given a brutal reminder of her situation.

I got punched; a knife in my head, my hair was pulled until it came out.

At night Marinela was taken back to the house in Edgbaston and kept there under lock and key. As the weeks turned into months, two more Romanian girls – both trafficked by Nejloveanu – arrived in Edgbaston. Marinela quickly realised that both had severe mental problems: the older one – she was 23 when she arrived – was later found to have a mental age of 10.

Even as the words form on the paper in front of me I am no longer in my little flat in Gateshead. I am no longer safe, my mum and my family around me: I see myself in Marinela's shoes. I see the room in Amsterdam where I was locked up, the window where I was forced to rent out my ravaged body to satisfy the callous lusts of men with enough disposable cash to abuse an already battered woman. I see me, I see Marinela, and I weep.

What happened next was also horribly familiar. Just as happened to me in Amsterdam and just as it happened to the girl on Oxford Street: Nejloveanu sold off some of his 'merchandise'. The two new girls made too little money for him, so he quickly sold them on to another pimp.

Marinela, meanwhile, was taken to one brothel after the next throughout the West Midlands. Of course the aim was to keep the customers happy with regular arrivals of new meat at their favoured sauna or massage parlour. In each, Marinela saw and worked alongside countless other Romanian women: she thinks that she met more than 100 in Birmingham alone. Many, though not all, had the same story as she did: kidnap, violence, threats and coercion.

And it wasn't just the West Midlands. In October 2008 she was shipped to Manchester, first to the Belle Air massage parlour and then to Shangri-La, both of them owned by David Greenwood. Marinela had no idea where she was being taken – it was just another grimy city suburb, just another sordid and shabby 'massage parlour'. She couldn't even think of escape: besides the regular beatings she endured she had no one she could trust and was terrified of what the police might do if she went to them. And she was right.

One day, shortly after she was taken to Manchester, the police raided Shangri-La. But they weren't looking for trafficked women, they weren't there to rescue anyone from sex slavery. Marinela and six other women were arrested, handcuffed and marched out of the red-brick building into a 'dog wagon' to be transported to the local police station.

The officers who arrested her were from Greater Manchester Police's sex crimes unit. She was treated as a prostitute and threatened with criminal charges. Even so, Marinela was grateful to them: that cold, rainy day in Manchester was the first time in more than six months when she hadn't been forced to have sex with a dozen men a day.

Normally, British police don't keep suspected prostitutes in custody. If they charge them, they do so fairly quickly, then spit them back out on to the streets. But Marinela wanted to stay locked up: she didn't want to leave the police station with its solid walls and big, reassuring locks. She was convinced that when she was released Nejloveanu and his gang would track her down and kill her.

Maybe that's what first caught the officers' attention. Because once they started to listen to Marinela's story they realised she wasn't just another prostitute: she was an innocent and brutalised victim of sex trafficking.

In the end, her story had a happy ending – or at least as happy as stories like this can have. Marinela was reunited with her family back in Romania. They had never given up the belief that she might be found – and found alive – but didn't know where to look or what to do. My mum says she knows how they felt. She too had come close to despair when I disappeared into Amsterdam's Red Light District, but she – like Marinela's family – never blew out the precious candle of hope.

Marinela settled in the north of England and worked as a part-time volunteer at a safe house for vulnerable women in Sheffield. She went to college to train as a hairdresser. When asked, she called herself a survivor, not a victim. And the men who trafficked and traded in Marinela's body were prosecuted, convicted and sent to prison for between four and 21 years.

But if you're thinking, as you read this, that it means everything is all right, then stop – because it isn't. Behind those trials and the comforting headlines about police smashing an international sex-trafficking gang – headlines splashed across national newspapers in 2009 – there is a different story. A very different – but sickening – story indeed. Let's start in Romania.

In the early hours of a May morning in 2009, officers from Alexandria Police received a tip-off from detectives in Manchester. The British police had been doggedly investigating Marius Nejloveanu and had discovered that far from being a lone – if vicious-trafficker, he was part of a criminal gang that shipped women into the sex trade throughout Europe. But this was no ordinary bunch of villains: it was a family-owned enterprise.

Together with his 51-year-old father Bogdan, Marius Nejloveanu worked to lure, kidnap, trick and traffic a string of Romanian girls, aged between 15 and 23 years old. After being raped – mostly by Marius – the women were shipped either to legal brothels in Spain or to the massage parlours and saunas that pollute British towns and cities. All were forced to work as prostitutes.

They didn't care how or where their victims came from – one of the girls was Marius Nejloveanu's own cousin – and they were ruthlessly brutal about ensuring they did as they were told. When, with the help of the tip-off from Manchester, Alexandria Police tracked down Nejloveanu to the nearby town of Mavrodin, they found the weapons he and his father had used to keep their victims in line: a heavy, wooden guitar was used to administer beatings, a knife to re-enforce threats of mutilation and murder.

Later Florea Stefan, the Chief Commissioner of Police, leant on the thick case file his detectives had built up and sighed: 'Marinela is lucky to be alive: many girls are beaten very, very badly. Nejloveanu exported five girls to the UK, but another seven have vanished in Romania. We don't know where they are, or if they are alive.'

Does that sound like a happy ending?

Let's return – for now – to England. Just before Christmas 2009, David Greenwood arrived back in Manchester. But he didn't come voluntarily: police had to take out a European arrest warrant to prise him from his luxurious bolt-hole – a villa paid for by the suffering of the women enslaved at his brothels – in Spain's Costa Del Sol.

When he appeared in court, Greenwood admitted to owning three brothels in Manchester: Belle Air, on the outskirts of the city centre, Cleopatra's in Bury and Shangri-La in Openshaw, where Mariela had been kept and raped up to 10 times a day. He openly told the court that he had run the businesses – which earned him hundreds of thousands of pounds a year – since 2006. That was how a former scaffolder could afford to live the high life in Spain.

But listen to what he – or rather his barrister – said next. Ms Elizabeth Jane Nicholls told the court that brothels in Greater Manchester 'operate with the co-operation of the police' and that her client had been 'led to believe that if these premises were run in a certain way there would be no prosecution'. And there was more: 'It is a truth that is undoubtedly universally known but little acknowledged in these courts that these parlours are well known to the police and operate with the co-operation of the police. What is effectively happening is de-facto licensing.'

She went on to say that 'Manchester is probably in a unique position' with a 'level of openness' between sex-sauna bosses and the authorities that 'plainly doesn't exist' throughout the country – and that Belle Air and Shangri-La had been known to the police for many years.

While there is an area of prostitution where people are exploited and forced into the trade, there has always been another side. One need only touch on the revelation of the highly educated and articulate lady, Belle de Jour.[1]

And then it got worse. Ms Nicholls told the court that the Inland Revenue had visited Greenwood's business because it filed annual tax returns. Tax returns? How could the Revenue justify pulling in taxes from the income of sex trafficking?

David Greenwood was eventually convicted of brothel keeping. He was sent to prison for 20 months.

I walked away from this story feeling ashamed. Ashamed that I too had once taken part in the running of a 'massage parlour' – if only briefly. But most ashamed that this vicious and uncaring sexual slavery seems to be so much a part of the warp and weft of British life that the Inland Revenue grab their slice and the police turn a blind eye. How could this be happening? What happened to me in Amsterdam should never have taken place, but at least you could give the Dutch government credit for not pretending that prostitution – in all its grubby, brutal forms – didn't happen.

In Britain we seem to want to reap the financial rewards of sex slavery while pretending it doesn't exist – even when it takes place in front of our eyes. Because it does; it really does. Just after the Nejloveanu and Greenwood verdicts, an investigation by senior police officers identified almost 5,890 saunas, massage parlours and venues illegally used for paid sex in England and Wales. How many? There aren't that many towns and cities in this country, yet we have nearly 6,000 brothels.

That investigation, by the Association of Chief Police Officers, also identified 342 brothels in the West Midlands alone. Remember the West Midlands? That's where Marinela was first trafficked to: according to ACPO statistics, she was just one among 1,535 Eastern European women working in brothels, each with an average of 6.6 beds. In Northwest England, 760 brothels were identified, employing 1,242 sex workers from Eastern Europe. And across the UK, ACPO found evidence that at least 400 women from Eastern Europe have been unwillingly trafficked, suffering a similar ordeal to Marinela's sex slavery.

I'm glad Marinela is free. I'm truly happy that she has found peace and safety, but the story behind her tale has re-kindled anger in me. If this is to stop, someone like me needs to make a difference. I must leave behind the grubby streets of Manchester and the leafy suburbs of Birmingham to start the next stage of my journey: I need to find out how and why so many thousands of women from Eastern Europe end up as sex slaves. If I am to know the whole 'elephant', not just its trunk or its tusks, I must – once again – find the courage to leave these shores.

---

[1] *Belle Du Jour* is the bestselling diary – alleged to be factual – of a British 'call-girl'. The author, Dr Brooke Magnanti, has repeatedly claimed that prostitution brought her only pleasure and wealth.

CHAPTER FIVE

THE SORROW OF BEAUTY

The first thing you notice is the sign outside the airport. 'Welcome to Chişinău – City of Potholes!' The second is the women: they are beautiful.

I'd never heard of Moldova. I had to look it up on a map to find out where it is. When at last I located it, tucked away on the edge of Europe, it looked tiny and insignificant. How on earth could this minuscule country be important in the vast global meat market of ăsex slavery?

Oh, but it is; it truly is.

Do something for me? Now, while the word is fresh on this page. Type 'Moldova' into Google and see what happens. See what I mean? Because somewhere, probably high up, on the first page of your Google search you'll also find the words 'women', 'sex' and 'trafficking'. Moldova is famous for all of them – very famous indeed.

Most countries – even the smallest and poorest, in the most underdeveloped parts of the world – have a number of products they export. Cotton, fruit, cereals, coffee at the bottom end of the scale, to cars, electronics and consumer goods for the better-off nations. Moldova has two exportable commodities: wine and women. Of the two, wine is the smaller.

Which is why we're on board a flight to Chişinău via Vienna (Moldova has no direct air links with most of Western Europe). It's four and a half hours across the Continent – and 50 years back in time.

You and I, we're going to meet young girls who have been trafficked into international sex slavery, the brave men and women who try to protect them – and, at the end of our trip, an international sex slaver. But first, let me tell you about this tiny backwater of a country called Moldova.

Draw a straight line running eastwards from London. Stop at Poland, the furthermost country in the European Union, then head south: pretty quickly you'll hit Romania. It's also in the EU, but the little landlocked country on the right isn't: you've now found Moldova.

Until 1991, Moldova, like its neighbours in the region, belonged to the USSR. When the Soviet Union collapsed that August, these little countries on the borders between Europe and Russia defiantly proclaimed independence. Moldova grabbed hold of its freedom within days of the Kremlin's rule imploding.

Those must have been heady times. Moldova had endured a miserable history of being annexed and plundered by (in turn) the Turkish Ottoman Empire, Imperial Russia, Royal Romania and the Communist USSR. By the time the Moldovan flag flew once again over the capital, Chişinău, its citizens had been the victims of foreign rule for more than 600 years.

'Freedom' is a word we bandy about all too freely in the comfortable, civilised, modernised West. In Britain we like to proclaim that we are the original home of freedom as a political idea. From the other side of the Atlantic, the United States appears to believe it can roll out the American model of freedom like Astro Turf across the difficult terrain of the Middle East.

But it's too precious a word to use so casually: throughout the months I was trapped in Amsterdam freedom was a dream – sometimes a mirage – which I clung to in the uttermost depths of despair and drug cravings. So what did freedom mean to Moldova? Something very different to what you might think.

The first thing it meant – of course – was freedom from the iron hand of Stalinist communism. For the first time in generations the people would be able to think freely and speak freely, without fear of their words landing them in some bestial Gulag in the USSR's frozen North. But the flip side to that shiny new coin was a different freedom: a 'freedom' from the financial security which came from being part of the Soviet Union. Before 1991, rigid communist rule meant that everyone (or at least almost everyone) had a job, a house, an income and the protection of a national health service. After 1991 Moldovans were free to starve, free to live on the streets because they couldn't afford the rapidly inflating rents, free to die for want of simple medicines.

Like I say, freedom is a tricky word.

But this is all ancient history, isn't it? What has this got to do with you? Why, in a book about sex slavery, do you have to read about the economic malaise of a small country, far, far away? Let me tell you.

Today, the population of Moldova is a little over 3.5 million. It used to be bigger – by about a quarter: nearly 900,000 Moldovans have left the country. Guess what happened to many of them? Ion Vizdoga – who devotes his life to helping trafficked women – knows. He said: 'Of all the countries in the world, Moldova is the one with the biggest number of its young women and girls sexually exploited abroad. Moldova is basically a source of victims of human trafficking. Thousands and thousands of young women – many of them mothers – have left Moldova and have been sexually exploited internationally.'

Talk to anyone in Moldova and the phrase you'll most often hear in conversation is '*cu parere*'. Translated from Romanian (the native language of most Moldovans), it means 'sorrowfully'. It precedes most statements about the country's plight, especially those focusing on the loss of its young women.

Ion Vizdoga leans forward and says: 'Sorrowfully, our women are beautiful and our country is poor.'

Sorrowfully, he's right – on both counts.

Take a walk through the heart of Chişinău, down the city's most important street, Stefan Cel Mare, and into Independence Square, and three things strike you straight away. The first is that it's the complete opposite of what you'd expect of the capital of a former Soviet country: instead of the stereotypical brutal concrete, the buildings in downtown Chişinău are old and beautiful. But the next thing you notice is that they are falling down, slowly but surely rotting away into dilapidation.

And then your eyes turn to the people walking past these lovely old structures. Chişinău is teeming with young people and the girls are breathtakingly tall, slim and, for the most part, blonde. In almost any other place in the world these young people would be an asset: in Moldova they are the country's curse.

Here, poverty – chronic, bitter poverty that means people don't have enough to pay their food bills, let alone get somewhere to live – has been driving the young generation abroad. Almost every young man and woman wants to find work outside Moldova. On TV, they see the apparent wealth and glamour of Western nations, compare this with the lack of jobs and money at home and make the decision to seek a better life elsewhere. Which, says Ion Vizdoga, is where the traffickers step in. 'It is impossible to live on the average monthly salary here of €100–150 per month. Because of this, everybody wants to go abroad and find a decent salary. Traffickers exploit this gap between normal life abroad and poverty in Moldova.'

Vizdoga is a big man, in every sense of the phrase. For a start he's tall – a little over six feet, with a solid build and a quiet – if intense – way of speaking that's immediately reassuring. But it's what he does – and has done for more than 15 years – that's more important. Because Ion Vizdoga fights, against overwhelming odds, to prevent Moldova's women from being sex-trafficked. He says: 'When in a village of 2,000 only 50 people have jobs, young people have two choices: commit crimes to survive, or leave the country and risk being trafficked.'

In 1991, when Soviet rule ended and the Iron Curtain was pulled aside, international sex traffickers soon saw a country full of tall, blonde, beautiful young women who could make them a fortune: the world over, they were exactly what people who seek out prostitutes were looking for. Add to that the fact that these women were desperate for money and the slavers knew they were on to a winner. They pounced on Moldova, just as 300 years earlier international slave traders descended on Africa.

International gangs, many from the former Yugoslavia and surrounding countries, set up shop in Chişinău. Many of them were already well established as drugs or guns traffickers. But a woman... now here was much better opportunity – with drugs you can only traffick them once because after that someone sticks them in their veins or snorts them up their nose. But a woman could still be trafficked and traded time after time: when she's no further use in one place, sell her on to the next.

Better yet, with Moldova still in the teething years of its independence there wasn't much in the way of an effective police force to worry about (and what did exist was often open to bribes to turn a blind eye), so it was easy to pose as a foreign businessman seeking women for domestic or childcare jobs abroad. Sounds familiar? That's how – half a world away – I ended up behind the windows in Amsterdam.

And Moldova's young women flocked to them. Lured by the promise of steady, well-paid (by Moldovan standards) jobs, they barely thought twice. The gangs smuggled them over the country's borders and then sold them on to brothels throughout Western Europe. Cities like Amsterdam, Paris and London found themselves with a new colony of foreign sex slaves.

At the time – and it's much the same today – Moldova didn't have much of a domestic prostitution industry but local criminals soon cottoned on to the trade. At the same time the international traffickers spotted a way to reduce their overheads: good capitalists one and all, they effectively franchised their operations to local 'businessmen'. The result was a new breed of Moldovan pimp – ready, willing and able to supply overseas 'clients'. In Chişinău the going rate for a new young sex slave was €500: once she was over the border, foreign traffickers could sell her for five times that amount in the West.

And that's how it works today – with just two differences. The first is that sex slavers, both local and domestic, have had the best part of 20 years to perfect their businesses, which now run with relentless efficiency. The second is that the price of a human being has dramatically dropped. Why? The supply of tall, beautiful and blonde young Moldovans seems inexhaustible.

People like Ion Vizdoga (and those from other countries who we'll meet later in this book) have a description for modern sex slaves: 'disposable people'. They are 'disposable' – like a Styrofoam coffee cup or a cheap biro – because they don't cost much in the first place. Have you ever met anyone who could be called 'disposable'? You're about to now.

The journey from Chişinău to Căuşeni takes about three hours and the road is just as advertised on that billboard at the airport – full of potholes. The city – more a town, really – is a sleepy, rural place; at the little bus station dogs pant in the midday heat while queues of locals wait for their ride to the outlying villages.

Early in 2011 Căuşeni bus station was the last comforting sight Cristina would have for a long time. At the age of 18 and barely out of school, she left the city with the promise of a bright new future. Here's her story – exactly as she told it, with tears streaming down her face in a hot dusty room in Căuşeni, several months later.

I was born in Căuşeni. Most of my family live here, but my cousin was in Chişinău and when I left school I hadn't seen her for a while. She had just had a baby – a little girl – so I decided I would go and visit them. Also, I needed work and I thought I could get work doing sewing or tailoring in Chişinău: I'm good at this sort of work.

And I did get work there doing tailoring. I worked during the day in a factory and at night I stayed with my cousin. One day I met a man – a local guy, from Chişinău: he asked me whether I was working or studying there. I told him I wasn't a student – I had a job, as a tailor.

He asked me how much I was earning and I told him between 1,500 and 2,000 leu [less than £100] a month. And he asked me, did I want to make more money than that? Of course I said yes — I wanted to take care of my parents, to send some money back home — but I couldn't do that on my salary. I also wanted to help myself a bit: to take care a little of my own life and maybe find somewhere of my own to live.

He said to me: 'If you want to work — and if you listen to me — you will have a lot of money in your life.' I asked him what he meant and he told me he would get me a good job outside Moldova. He said: 'If you want, I can make your documents for this: I can make all your documents in one week and then you will go abroad'.

I asked where I would go and he said Cyprus: Turkish Cyprus. I said yes straight away. It sounded exciting and I asked him how much I would be paid; he said I would get a lot of money. So I asked him what work I was going to do and he said that I would work in 'consultation'.[1]

He said that I would work in a café or a bar. My job would be to sit with a customer and drink tea, or coffee or a glass of champagne — that was all there was to it. He never told me I would have to do something else, something awful.

I agreed, and the next day he got me a passport. Then he got me a visa to go to Cyprus. He didn't tell me how much this cost him, how much money he had to pay. He just handed me my passport. I looked at it and there was my photo in it. But then he took my passport back from me. He told me it was to keep it safe. On the third day he took me to the airport. He gave me passport with the visa, some air tickets and $5. He told me this was to buy a bottle of water.

My plane flew from Chişinău to Istanbul. I had to change to another plane there to get to Cyprus. It was very confusing and it was very difficult to find my way, but I managed somehow.

When I got off the plane I was met by a man. I didn't know his name — he didn't introduce himself. He took me to a room somewhere, I don't know where. In there were seven other girls. The man said we would be taken to hospital the next day for a medical check up.

We all slept in the room that night. There was no light in the room; the man locked us in. None of us knew where we were — we didn't know anything. The next day the man came and took us to a hospital and we were 'verified'. I didn't know what that meant.

After we were verified, men came and took girls away: each man would take two girls or one girl — it seemed to depend on what they agreed between themselves. We didn't speak the language and we didn't know what was happening.

A man took me to a building somewhere — he said it was a casino. I was given a glass of Coca-Cola and a cigarette. And the man asked me, 'Do you know why you are here?' Of course I said yes: I was to work in consultation. But really he meant I was to be a prostitute. At the time I didn't realise that: I knew only what the man in Chişinău had told me — that I would sit with people at a table and drink a glass of champagne or something, and that I would be paid for this.

After 20 minutes or maybe half an hour he said: 'You are on the clock.' I didn't understand what he meant by this. Then a Russian girl came into the room and said I should go with her. She said she was on the clock, too.

We sat down. Two old men came to sit with us and we drank a glass of champagne. Then the Russian girl got up with one of the old men. I asked her why she was leaving me there with the other one. She said: 'You have to have sex with him.'

I was in shock; I said that I didn't want to, but she said: 'It doesn't matter if you want to or not — you have to do it.' I was terrified but she told me that if I didn't do this, the boss would beat both of us. I had to let the old man have sex with me.

Afterwards I was crying and felt so dirty. I had a bath and tried to sleep but I couldn't. All that night I lay there thinking of what had happened: I wanted to die.

The next day I told the Russian girl to speak to the boss for me. I asked her please to tell him that there was a mistake and I wanted to go home. But she didn't want to: she said if she told him this, he would be violent to her or might not give her any money, and that it would all be my fault. So I asked one of the other girls to tell the boss: she agreed to translate for me. I told him that I wanted to go back to Moldova; that I had been tricked into coming here and had not known that I would be a prostitute. If I had, I would never have come — never, ever would I have come.

The boss looked at me. He just said: 'It is too late for you to go home now. You have been paid for. You will stay here and make men happy.'

That day they brought me more men. I had to let them have sex with me. The first man, he didn't do anything to me. Anything, anything. He put me on the bed and saw that I was crying. He told me to get some sleep and then he just left. The second man took his pleasure with me and walked out. I waited for the next one.

When he came in, I told him I did not want to do this with

97

him; I told him I just wanted to go home, to Moldova. He began beating me until I gave in. Six or seven men that day made me have sex with them. And the same again the next day. It was terrible. Whoever chose me could have me. They paid the boss to do sex to my body.

On the day after that the boss man brought me a piece of paper to sign. It was in Turkish language and I didn't understand it. A girl from the casino came and translated it to me: she said: 'It is for the police — you have to sign this and say you agree to stay here for half a year to practise prostitution.'

I refused to sign it. I kept saying that I wanted to go back to Moldova, that there had been a mistake. I started crying and crying — I cried so much. But they would not listen. The boss man took me back to the casino and they kept making me have sex with men; five, six or seven men every day.

Every day the boss made me do sex with these men: he said that I had a huge debt to him because he had paid for my passport, my visa and my air tickets. After a week I had not been eating at all. I had only tea, whisky and cigarettes — I could not eat food. Then I became friends with one of the other girls there. She was a very good girl — she tried to help me. I am thankful to her. I told her that I wanted to go back to Moldova. I said: 'If I don't go to Moldova, I will kill myself here and death would take me to Moldova. I will cut my veins or take pills. I will find some way to do it. It is better to go home dead, than to let someone abuse me. And my body.'

She helped me get out of that place, to escape. And she led me to the police station so I could tell my story. The policeman got someone to translate because I could not speak

Turkish. Then he gave me three papers to sign to make me go home to Moldova. I was so happy – I was going to get away.

But then someone from the casino telephoned to find out if I was there. The other girls must have told the boss. The police said the boss wanted me back because there were clients waiting to have me. They took me back to the casino and told me I must do sex with the men; I had no choice. But they told me I would be free the next day; they said they would come to the casino and take me to the airport and I would go home. But they did not come the next day, or the day after that. On the third day, they still did not come.

All those days the boss made me have sex with the men who wanted to abuse me. I tried to say no but the boss and his men beat me. Then on the fourth day the police came for me.

They took me to the airport. They didn't give me money – they gave me only the tickets and they said, 'You're going home.'

I arrived at four in the morning in Istanbul airport. But I was told that I had to pay for visa: 30 dollars, or 35, I don't know. I didn't have this money. I started to cry – I thought I would be sent back to Cyprus and made to do sex again with the boss's customers. I sat on a bench and I cried. I didn't know what to do, where to go. Who could I tell that I don't have money to go to Moldova?

A man who was walking by came up to me. He said he would pay the money for my visa. Then he said: 'Come with me.' I thought he was going to show me where to wait for the plane to Chişinău, but he took me to a taxi. Two other men came with us, they were holding my arms.

The taxi driver took us to a flat. The men made me go inside, then they tied me to the bed. I said: 'No, no, no!' But they just tied me down; they tied my hands and legs and then they took my clothes off me. And they raped me. I cried, but they said they knew I was a prostitute so I had to have sex with them.

When they had finished, they took me back to the airport and left me. I was in a very bad condition – I don't remember how I got through the big corridors with all the people. I tried to watch to see someone with a blue Moldova passport, but I didn't see any. Then I heard some women speaking Romanian: it was a mother and a girl. I ran to them and said: 'Are you from Moldova? Are you going to Chişinău?'

That was how I found my way to the plane: the woman and the girl helped me. They also let me use their phone to call my cousin: she was surprised to hear from me but she said she would meet me at the airport in Chişinău.

When we landed in Chişinău I was so happy. I wanted so much to get down off the plane that I fell down the steps on to the ground. But I didn't care – I was so very happy to be back in Moldova.

At security there were some policemen. When I saw them I began crying and shaking badly. I remembered the policemen in Cyprus. They asked me where I had been and I told them the whole story, of how I had been tricked and sent to prostitution. They were very kind and they told me bad guys were hanging around in the airport. They said they looked out for girls like me – girls on their own, who looked vulnerable. They said they would wait in the big hall near the exit and if I saw any guy I didn't know coming towards me, I was to give them a special sign by waving my scarf. Then they would come and get him.

When I got through the control of passports I saw my cousin. I ran to her and threw myself into her arms. I said: 'Please take me home, don't leave me alone ever again.' I was so happy.

But when we got outside there was the guy who had sent me to Cyprus. He was waiting for me; my cousin must have told him. He was angry. He asked me why I had come back and said he had spent much money to send me to Cyprus. He pushed me towards his car. I looked for the policemen and I was going to give my sign to them, but my cousin was holding me so tightly that I couldn't wave my scarf. I was in the car and I started crying as this guy started the engine. I thought: 'Now he will kill me and I will never go back home to see my family.'

But suddenly the policemen knocked at the car window. They said we needed to go to the police station with them. It was 11pm and until four the next morning they asked me questions and got me to tell them everything that had happened to me.

At the end they gave me some food and told me I need not be afraid any more. They said they had arrested the man who had sold me to the people in Cyprus. The next day I was able to go home to C u eni. But I could not tell my parents what had happened to me: it would have been too much a shame for them in our town. And today I still not like to eat – I am scared and worry that the man who sent me to Cyprus will come with his friends and kill me.

Cristina wiped away another tear and pointed towards the door. The interpreter said she needed to go outside for a cigarette. As she stepped on to the pavement she suddenly collapsed: her legs buckled, her eyes rolled up into her head and she fell – half of her tiny body on the paving stones, half on the road. A social worker, who was with her throughout the interview, lifted her back inside and brought her some water. She smiled a tight, thin, resigned smile: 'Sorrowfully, this happens to Cristina when she tells her story.'

There are Cristinas everywhere in Moldova. Young, beautiful women whose only 'crime' was to hope for something better in their lives and believe a man when he promised it to them in another country. What's worse is that there is a real culture of shame in Moldova (and in many countries like it). Cristina didn't dare tell her family what had happened because they would all be viewed as almost unclean. On top of that, Moldova is too poor to have any proper centres for helping the thousands of victims like Cristina. Instead it's left to voluntary organisations, who do their best but cannot cope with the number of women who have been tricked and trafficked into international sex slavery.

Ion Vizdoga knows this only too well: he was once a public prosecutor but for the past decade has run one of the voluntary agencies, the Centre for the Prevention of Trafficking in Women. Personally, he has worked with more than 200 women trafficked out of the country and into Western brothels. As he sheltered from the sun under one of Chişinău's many trees, he wiped his brow and sighed:

'In Moldova, trafficked and exploited victims return with hundreds of problems related to their medical, social, family and financial condition. They went abroad to earn money, but come back to Moldova with only troubles. As a result, in most of the cases these young women are abandoned by their husbands, children, parents, simply because it is known that they have been sexually exploited.'

And maybe that explains the next thing I found shocking: some – indeed many – of these women aren't trafficked just the once but twice and sometimes three times.

An hour's drive away from Chişinău, Natalia is sitting on a bed in an overcrowded hostel for trafficked women. She shares her room with three other girls – all are around 25, the same age as her. But Natalia looks much older, very much older indeed. And I know why.

She shakes, physically: her hands, her legs are in constant movement. Her face twitches and twists, too. I know these signs. I have been where she is now: a drug addict, she is rattling badly. This is her story.

I was born in Căinari. This is a big town, 45 kilometres from Chişinău. In Soviet times it was a rich town, because it was on the main railway for Moldova and many goods come through. But when independence came there were no jobs and we were six children in our family. It was difficult – very difficult – for money. All of us wanted to help our parents. When I left school, I tried to get work but there was none. Eventually I spoke to a woman in the town about how I could go abroad to do jobs. She said she could send me to Turkey.

I asked her what work I could do there. She told me I would be cleaning in hotels; she said she would arrange the ticket and the visa, and I would pay her back from the money I would earn. The next day after we talked, she gave me the ticket. I travelled to Turkey the following day.

When I got to Istanbul I was met by two men; they took me to a house. They said: 'This is where you work.' I asked what cleaning I do and they laughed: they said there was no cleaning — I was to make sex with men, Turkish men. Of course, I made a big argument but they beat me — they beat me hard. But still I refuse so they sold me to some other guy.

The same thing happened again: I refused to be prostitute and I was beaten. Three more times that happen until the last time when I could not fight any more and I had to do sex with the men who my boss brought to me. The men were horrible. Dirty, stinking men who wanted just to fuck me: I was crying so much but they didn't care. They paid the boss and fucked me.

For a month and a half this is what happened to me. Every day, seven, eight, 10 men took what they wanted from me but my boss said I was no good — I didn't earn enough money — so he beat me. Then he sold me to someone else. The same story. More men; more dirty, hard fucking — it hurt me so much. And always after a week, maybe two, I was sold to another boss. Each one say the same thing: he has paid money for me so I must earn money to pay him back.

One day I escape. I was in a room on the second floor. I climb out of the window and on to a roof. Then I jumped from the roof into a tree — that hurt, but I was desperate to get away. I climbed down the tree and ran into the street. I look everywhere and run and run. Then I saw a police car and I stopped it: I kept saying 'problem, problem' over and over in Romanian language.

This police, they were good. They took me to the police place and made me wait. A man came in who speak Romanian and I told him what happened to me. The police told me I was safe: they bought me air ticket and took me to the airport in Istanbul.

When I arrived in Chişinău I was so happy but I could not go home: none of my family knew what had happened to me, I could not tell them. So I stayed in Chişinău, hoping to find work. I look in the newspaper and I see a notice for a business which arranged jobs in England: it was to look after babies. Of course I was suspicious; I am not stupid. I did not know if this was true job or if it would be like the last time. So I went to see the business. It was in the big hotel – Hotel Chişinău.[2]

Although Natalia did not know it, the building now housed numerous bogus recruitment companies.

A woman spoke to me – she said it was true job, good job – no sex or prostitution. She promised me. The woman told me I would have to pay for my documents – passport, visa and plane ticket – but I said I had no money. I explained what had happened to me. The woman went away to speak to her boss. When she came back, she said that to help me the boss had agreed to lend me the money to pay for my documents; she said I would have to pay it back from my wages in England. She said I would have good money so it would be no problem.

I stayed at the house of the woman for three days while my documents were prepared. She was good to me: she gave me food and told me about what it would be like in England. And I thought that at last I was going to have some good luck.

On the fourth day, three men came to the apartment. One, who was from Moldova, said they would take me to the airport — but they did not.

When we got out outside they pushed me in the back part of the car, where cases are normally put, and they shut the lid down tight. I was scared, so scared, and I cried out — but no one could hear me.

I do not know for how long we drove. I had no watch and anyway, it was dark in the place where they put me. It smelled so bad and I think I slept or something. I do not remember too much.

When the car stopped, the men pulled me from my place. One had a gun and pushed it at me. The man, who was Moldovan, said that I had been bought and that I was to work for them, making money by having sex with men. I could not say no: it was dark and I did not know what country I was in, whether I was in Moldova or some other place. I thought I was going crazy: how can this happen to me two times? I thought maybe I had done something to make God angry and He was punishing me.

The men took me inside a place. I thought I was to have some sleep, but the men pushed me on the floor and they raped me, one after the other. They took turns to push themselves inside me and have their pleasure. I cried and asked them: 'Please stop, it is hurting my body.' But they did not.

The next day and the day after we drove. The men said it was OK for me to sit in the seats in the car because I knew that if I tried to escape, they would shoot me. Can I tell you how it feels to be like that? Your mind closes and you cannot do anything except what you are told. I could not move. I sat in the car and thought that everything was my fault because I had agreed to do this job in England and I should know better.

There came a day when the car stopped and the men took me to a bar in a little street. I did not know where I was. In the bar people spoke the same as the two men who were not from Moldova. They sat with a man — he was ugly, with a big head with no hair. I saw him give the two men some money, a big amount of notes. Then they and the man from Moldova got up and walked to the door. The Moldovan man said I belonged to the one with the bald head now. I asked him, 'Where am I, please?' He said it was Albania. Then they left me.

The bar had some rooms above it on number one floor. The bald man showed me there, then he pulled off my jeans and he raped me. After, he told me this was where I had to work.

I think I stay in this place for two months. Each day men come to have sex with me. They were very hard to me: if I did not please them in every way, they would hit me and beat me. One time, one man was so cruel I went unconscious. But when I was awake, the bald man said I had to work and more men came to take my body.

One day the bald man, he say that we have to leave. We get in his car and he drives to the sea. Then he sells me to another man: he is my new boss and we get on a boat to go over the water.

Natalia is shaking. Now her eyes are wide and hunt from side to side. Her skin is reddening and she has begun to sweat – this is a very bad 'rattle'. And I know – oh, how I know – the pain she is going through. But there is no help for it: here in this shelter she has just one chance and that depends on staying clean of drugs. Besides, her story is not yet finished – not by a long way.

Natalia's journey across Europe was almost a blueprint for modern sex trafficking: smuggled by boat to Italy and imprisoned in a brothel before being driven across the border to France and sold to new slave-owners. Used and abused in France and then Belgium before being sold again, and trafficked to Amsterdam.

As soon as she said the word – even in Romanian – I knew it. And I knew how and why she was rattling.

She had begun to use drugs in Italy – soft ones at first, cannabis and hashish. Just like me, the long sweet draughts of marijuana smoke had helped dull the pain of being raped over and over. But in Amsterdam, cocaine quickly took the place of cannabis.

I did not work in the windows there; that was not for me. My boss in Amsterdam made me work in a private brothel. It was in a house, closed off from the street. A woman was there, who took the money from men and also told the boss if I did not do what the men wanted.

One day I could not: I was in hurt [pain] so much and I wanted to lie and rest. But the boss man came and beat me: he punched me in my face and one of my teeth fell out. I did not dare to say no again.

I work in that place for eight months. I do not know how many men had sex with me – I think thousands. The woman who took the money also brought me drugs. I needed to smoke them because it helped me to go away in my head while the men entered me. One day she give me a different drug – it was on top of a plastic bottle of Cola. She heated the drug with a lighter and told me to breathe in the smoke.

I was so sick straight away – very, very sick. But the smoke made less pain for me when men had sex with my body. I wanted it all the time because the men came to use me all the time. Now I need it so bad.

Natalia's ordeal in the brothel was so like the year I endured in Amsterdam's Red Light District: she had been tricked, raped, sold and then raped and sold again and again. Like me, she had ended up as a crack whore, deliberately fed a drug that would – more effectively than even the beatings – imprison her in the brothel.

Her time there only ended when Dutch police raided the house. Unlike the windows in the Red Light District, it was not licensed by the City Council. But instead of treating Natalia as a victim, the police put her in a cell and then sent her home to Moldova.

Here in the overcrowded shelter, with little help to overcome her years of sex slavery and none to help her get off drugs, she sat shaking and sobbing. All hope had left her eyes, which were dull and lifeless. When asked what she believed would happen to her now, she shrugged.

I do not know. I cannot go back to my family – there is too much shame for them to know what happened to me. Sorrowfully, I do not think there is any life for me now.

The more you look at countries like Moldova – and the more you meet its women, who have been tricked and trafficked abroad – the more you come to realise that what makes them such easy prey for sex slavers is just one word: poverty. According to the European Union, Moldova itself is the poorest country on the continent. And its people – especially the women, who for a variety of cultural reasons often have less chance of a job at home than men – are simply desperate.

Ana Revenco is a tall, elegant woman; she sits in a first-floor room in a cramped office building a little way outside the centre of Chişinău. Her face is drawn with tiredness and her voice is weary. As well it might be: because she runs La Strada Moldova, one of the few organisations devoted to both helping victims of trafficking and to stopping the trade in the first place. She smokes, steadily and with purpose, and chooses her words with care: 'Ten years ago, the traffickers began putting adverts in newspapers, offering "jobs for young nice-looking women, good pay, passport needed, visa arranged, nice, good-looking, no experience or foreign language needed". And many, many women responded and fell for this trick.

'Over the next few years the adverts became less direct in their message – more intelligent, if you want. Typically they would just say "jobs abroad, well paid jobs" so they didn't appear to be directly aimed at women. But people –

both men and women – responded anyway, and it was easy for the traffickers to be able to select only the women when they called them on the phone.'

Ana picks up a newspaper from a pile on her desk. It looks like one of those free advertising papers that are pushed, once a week, through everyone's letterboxes at home. Called *Makkler*, it is in fact published twice a week in Chişinău. It's also where most of today's trafficking adverts are published. Ana points to the classified columns and a typical advert.

'Here is one which says it is looking for young women to take jobs as dancers in Japan, Thailand and Italy. It is immediately suspicious because it promises to pay for the women's air tickets, their visas and their accommodation. And the salary is $2,000 per month: that is around 15,500 or 25,000 leu – more than 10 times the monthly salary of a person in Moldova.'

You know what strikes me about that advert? It's almost identical to the one that got me trapped in sex slavery. Substitute 'nursery nurse' for the word 'dancer' and it's the same – and with exactly the same result.

La Strada Moldova operates a free telephone hotline for women to call if they become suspicious about a job offer they've been given; it takes dozens of calls a week and has, at any one time, around 28 active cases. Some are from women who have already fallen prey to sex traffickers and find themselves trapped as prostitutes in a foreign country; others stem from parents and relatives desperate to trace daughters who have disappeared after signing up to work abroad.

To find out more about how this trafficking worked, we

answered one of the adverts in Makkler. With the help of a local journalist, posing as a young girl desperate for a job, we arranged an interview with the person who had placed the ad. I'd assumed it would be a man and that we would have to go to an office. But the advertiser turned out to be a young and attractive woman, who called herself Olga. She wanted to meet on a street outside a café on the other side of Chişinău – at 9pm. Ana Revenco was instantly on her guard.

'This is, of course, very suspicious. If you are to seek employment here in Moldova, you will never meet with a future employer or with an agency that is mediating employment, you will never meet on the street.

'Let me tell you one more thing, why they meet at night. In the daytime people have their alert system on more. In the evening people tend to relax – have a beer, have a coffee – and they dream. So it is easier for a trafficker to manipulate someone: whatever they want to plant in the hand of the woman who applies to them will have more chance to succeed because she is already hopeful and her alert system will not ask the really important questions.'

With Ana's warnings in mind, we set out to meet Olga. Using a hidden camera, our local journalist recorded exactly what she said. Read it – and make up your own mind.

Reporter: So, what's the job?

Olga: It is in Syria. We've been in Syria for six months and you should know, it's very good. It's a cabaret club. So, you dance, dance, and then sit at the table with the clients.

Reporter: What do you have to do with clients?
Olga: Nothing, you talk to them. There are other clubs which are striptease clubs, and clubs where there are prostitutes but this club is different.

You should know that you will have money already in your first day at work. Besides your salary, you receive money every day, from the first day. For example, you sit at a table with a client for two hours. For two hours, you get 10 dollars.

And you know, they are nice. For example, I have guys who send me money up until today. Honestly, I swear to God. Because, to be honest, they're stupid. They are afraid of women like us, you know? You sit with him at the table for half an hour and he falls in love. He can give you even his entire house, you know?

There is a bodyguard at the club and the boss is very good – awesome, very kind, honestly. He has worked for 25 years with girls from Russia, Ukraine. But when clients come, everybody asks: 'Do you still have girls from Moldova?'
Reporter: But what if, for example, a client goes to the patron and tells him: 'I like this girl and I want to take her and sleep with her'?
Olga: This has never happened to us, it doesn't happen – it's all a game, a game in which you always win and always choose. You choose what you want, and whether you want or not to stay at his table.

So, if you give me tomorrow a copy of your passport and two small pictures that is all I need. I will send them to the boss; he will get the visa and send you the ticket. He pays for it all, yes, but I guess that afterward you pay him back the money for the ticket.

Also, I don't think that you will go alone. I'm still looking for girls and I would like to send more in a group, so that you're not alone. The thing is that now the club is closed for renovation, they change something there, and the boss told me to find 20 girls, and then to talk to him; and so now I help him.

What do you think? Does this sound like a legitimate job interview? I know what *I* think – and Ana Revenco has seen this all too often to be fooled. She wasn't surprised when we passed the details on to her. 'Traffickers paint a rich, happy future to trap their victims. They try to give specific examples so the person actually starts to believe inside; they try and materialise the money that she hasn't even started to make in an apartment. So she's there, she's most probably young and when you are young you don't have life skills, social skills, employment, experience. And she hears all these positive stories and she falls in the trap.'

Maybe you're thinking, how do they get away with it? If it's so obvious, why doesn't someone – the government, the police – do something to shut the traffickers down? It's a good question. But to find the best way to show you, we'll have to leave Chişinău again.

It doesn't take long to get out of the city. And once you leave its tree-lined streets and constant traffic congestion, you take a step back in time. Imagine the countryside near you – and then rewind by 60, 70 or 80 years. That's what rural Moldova looks like. Families here work the land as they always have done, often by hand or with wheezing ancient Soviet tractors. This isn't just poor, it's dirt poor.

Traffickers, as we've seen, exploit that poverty by preying on the hopes and dreams of young women, but there's another side to it they also turn to their advantage: hand in hand with poverty goes corruption.

Ion Vizdoga used to prosecute traffickers: in all he has dealt with more than 700 cases. But only a very few of them were sent to prison: 'Sorrowfully, only 10 per cent of all defendant traffickers have been convicted and therefore serve their criminal sentence. The reason for this is corruption. Most of the time only simple, low-level traffickers are convicted. High-level traffickers – the ones who run the big operations – are not really in the sights of law enforcement, because such traffickers usually operate under the protection of law enforcement itself.'

Three hours' drive northwards from Chişinău, a pair of rusty and battered metal gates, joined to the stone buildings around them with some ancient iron-work and topped with haphazard barbed wire, are the only sign that we have arrived at one of Moldova's higher security prisons. This part of the country feels very different to the South: it is home to Moldova's minority Russian population, a legacy from Stalin's rule.

Behind the barbed wire, inside a tiny visitors' room, a bulky middle-aged Russian man waits. His name is Alexandr Kovali and he is both an international sex-trafficker and living proof of the corruption that allows men like him to operate. Kovali is more usually known in Moldova by his Russian nickname of 'Salun' – 'joker' or 'play-actor' – and he's unquestionably good at playing the part of an innocent man. But the reality behind the mask is anything but a joke. To meet 'Salun' Kovali is to encounter evil.

Kovali started out as a soldier – almost certainly a mercenary – in the bloody and massacre-ridden Balkan Wars of the early 1990s. He fought for Serbia, a country whose most senior military officers and politicians are accused of war crimes and ethnic cleansing. When the wars finally ended, he found himself out of work.

'We were defeated; Yugoslavia was defeated. So when I was about to leave, the guys, my Serbs, advised me to open a nightclub in Romania. So, together with a Romanian guy, I opened a nightclub. After two years of work there, I saw that there were no nightclubs in Moldova so I came here, to Chişinău.

'I opened a club here. I got approval for selling tobacco and alcohol. And then I opened a second club. But people think that a nightclub must involve crime in some way. This is because Hollywood dictates the way we see nightclubs. All mafia meetings shown in the movies take place in nightclubs. If someone wants to buy drugs, they go to a nightclub.

'Unfortunately for Hollywood directors it doesn't happen like this in Moldova. Moldova is too poor to trade in drugs – nightclubs or no nightclubs. Of course in my clubs there were girls. They were working in consummation.[3] That is where they earned their money. What they did after the

116

clubs closed at 5am is none of my business – this is their private life.'

Kovali bangs the table with the side of his hand as he speaks. He is fluent and conversational, punctuating his speech with rhetorical questions. but he is also a shameless liar. In 2006 he was charged with importing women – some were just girls of 15 – to work as prostitutes in his clubs. Once they were 'broken in', he then sold many of them to work as sex slaves in countries as far afield as Russia, Israel, Turkey and all across Western Europe. His business turned him into one of the richest men in the country.

Ion Vizdoga was part of the team who brought Alexandr Kovali to justice. Throughout the trial, he supported 'Salun's' victims. When he recalls them, a shadow passes across his face: 'He was very violent towards his victims. He shaved their heads and punished any of them who would not do what he told them to. They were threatened, blackmailed, beaten, raped, and kept in cellars. He is a very, very dangerous man.'

At the end of his trial, Kovali was sentenced to 19 years' hard labour, which is why he is sitting in this small room in the remote prison in the north of Moldova. But it was what happened next which was most revealing.

Kovali appealed against his conviction and in January 2007 strode in to Chişinău's court building flanked by burly minders. The court process required his victims to once again give evidence against him: to stand in the witness box facing their trafficker and repeat the stories of what he had done to them. I know how this feels; how much it hurts to face a sex-slaver: I had to do so when the man who trafficked me to Amsterdam's Red Light District was prosecuted in England. But he was a low-level sex-slaver whereas Alexandr Kovali was a rich and powerful man, with friends in high places.

Sitting in the quiet shade of a peaceful garden, Ion Vizdoga recalls what happened next. 'At this hearing there was the risk of Salun being set free. One of the victims I was working with, who gave testimony against him, made two suicide attempts. She was so scared of having to see him that she tried to even cut her throat just to avoid meeting Salun face to face.'

Imagine the desperation of a young woman – a girl – who has already been trafficked, raped, beaten and brutalised. Imagine the vicious, blinding terror that made her take a knife to her throat. I can imagine this – oh, how I can.

As the appeals court considered Kovali's case, the man himself walked out into the street. A local photographer tried to take his picture. Immediately Kovali's minders stopped him and the journalist was threatened with being locked up by police. The message was not lost on Moldova's supposedly free press: 'Salun' had protection – and protection in very important places.

In Russian, the word for such protection is 'krysha'. Literally translated, it means 'a roof'. According to Ion Vizdoga, Kovali used to pay his krysha – an official in the police ministry – €100,000 a year to be allowed to run his businesses. It was only when the official left his post that Kovali was arrested.

The court eventually dismissed Kovali's appeal: his 19-year sentence was upheld. Outraged, Kovali himself wrote by hand a 20-page statement laying out, in great detail, his corrupt relationship with the Moldovan police. But worse than that he implicated the deputy director of a new and high-profile unit called the Centre for Combating Trafficking in Persons.

The Centre had been launched in a blaze of international publicity a year before Kovali's arrest. It was paid for by a $1.9 million grant from the American government. The deputy director had been praised throughout Europe and the US as Moldova's 'one good cop'. Now he was being accused by an international sex-trafficker of corruptly giving protection.

And then a strange thing happened. Kovali received an 'important visitor in his cell'. He then retracted his allegations. Ion Vizdoga shakes his head: 'This is true; this is all true. "Salun" Kovali named seven collaborators from the Centre for Combating Trafficking in Persons. All were police officers who were supposed to stop this trade in women but nothing has happened to them.

'Today, there are lots of "Saluns", who are free and live well. We can see those police collaborators who, after three, four, five years of work, afford buying luxurious apartments, luxurious cars and houses, when their salary is in fact very small. I suspect that about 50 per cent of illegal profits, obtained as a result of selling and exploiting victims of human trafficking, are in the pockets of corrupt people.'

Sorrowfully – as Moldovans say – the evidence supports Ion Vizdoga.

In 2006 the world's largest intergovernmental body, The

Organization for Security and Cooperation in Europe (www.osce.org), monitored sex-trafficking trials in Chişinău for six months.

I found the report online: you can, too – and I think you should because whole sections are truly terrible. Try this – it's a report of one trafficking case observed by the OSCE monitors: 'The district court judge appeared to fall asleep after resting his head on the Criminal Code lying on his desk. The defendant quickly took advantage of the situation to threaten the victim with non-verbal hand gestures, simulating cutting her throat.'

Tell me something: if you were a young woman who had been tricked, threatened raped and repeatedly abused – and if the man who did this to you was able to threaten you in court – would you be brave enough to give evidence against him? I don't know if I would. Would you trust in the common sense and fairness of the judges? At another trafficking trial, the judge told the OSCE observers: 'These young ladies are prostitutes: they go abroad and prostitute themselves, then they are not happy with the money they get, so upon their return, they complain they were trafficked. But I know their kind, I've seen their pictures – they're all smiling while dancing, and then they say that they were trafficked.'

Some people who read my previous book questioned whether sex-traffickers would be allowed to sell women from one country to the next, trading in their flesh and making money from their misery. Now you've read what the judge said, do you have an answer?

And it's not just the judges. According to Ion Vizdoga,

Moldovan police are notorious not only for protecting traffickers and pimps (he claims many of the biggest local pimps are themselves policemen), but for demanding sexual favours from those women who dare to complain. As he says this, my mind travels from Chişinău to Amsterdam: in my Red Light Hell, I was raped by seven police officers – men who were meant to be protecting women. They knew these were 'freebies' – sexual bribes given by the pimps (but forced on girls like me) to ensure nothing disturbed their lucrative businesses.

Even when a good cop – and there are some, everywhere – defies this bitter corruption, the sheer economics of sex slavery take over.

Remember Ana Revenco, earlier in this chapter? La Strada Moldova – the organisation she heads up – employs psychotherapists to work with the victimised women and to teach local police how to take statements from them. Alina Budeci is one of them: 'You can have a policeman who spends years trying to catch a local Mafioso, and he finally puts all the evidence together and the guy is convicted and sentenced. And the next day he comes to the police station: "Look at me, I am free. I paid €40,000 for my freedom." The policeman in such a case is heartbroken.'

We have spent a long time, you and I, in this small forgotten corner of the world. Here, we have met women – girls like me: tricked and trafficked, beaten and raped – and we have met those who try to help them. And we have met a rich and unrepentant trafficker. Why, I know you are asking, why have we spent so long here? What is Moldova to me? What is it to you, Sarah Forsyth? However terrible, why does the plight of women there matter in the bigger picture of international sex slavery?

And I'll tell you. It matters because these brutal men and these poor, beaten women are not just a problem for Moldova. Oh no, far from it. Remember, Moldova is the biggest exporter of women into prostitution worldwide. From the Far East to the Middle East, from southern Europe to town and cities throughout Britain. Yes, Moldova is now free.

It's free to export its most precious asset. Sorrowfully.

---

[1] The actual Romanian word used was 'consultatie' but in Moldova this is often confused with the word 'consumatie'. There is no direct English translation of this, but the nearest equivalent would probably be 'hostess'.

[2] Hotel Chişinău is a big, imposing building on one of the main streets in the City, with offices as well as rooms for hire.

[3] Kovali spoke in Russian, but 'consummation' is the equivalent of the Romanian 'consumatie', meaning 'hostess'.

CHAPTER SIX

THE APPLIANCE
OF SCIENCE

Where's the best place to hide something? The answer: in plain sight.

Think for a minute. There is something which each one of us sees every day of our lives. It's probably the most common and ubiquitous part of our daily lives, yet we rarely, if ever, notice it: it's the barcode.

The idea was invented more than 60 years ago: a simple, digital code with a unique 'identity' for every object, which allows the owner to evaluate sales and keep track of merchandise with a simple swipe. The first consumer goods to carry a barcode were little packets of Wrigleys' chewing gum. Now it's on just about everything we buy – even this book has a barcode printed on the back.

So why, in a book about sex slavery, are we talking about barcodes? We'll get to that.

Trafficking human beings is a business. No, more than that, it's an industry – a vast commercial enterprise that's an inextricable part of today's globalised economy. The United Nations reckons it earns around $32 billion a year.

Of course it's not a legal industry: there's no country on the planet which allows the trafficking in human beings, but that's theory, and the practice is pretty much the opposite. Black market trading in human beings is flourishing and the occasional success stories in breaking up trafficking networks are really no more than a few drops in a very large ocean indeed.

The people who profit from trafficking are businessmen. And like all successful businessmen, they pay attention to the latest trends in the marketplace. Their trade may be despicable but traffickers are generally smart and the smartest rule in any business is to target low-risk, high-reward ventures. Selling women for sex hits those targets every time.

Why? Because there's a depressingly scientific equation involved in any business. Demand must either meet or exceed supply, and supply must constantly be refreshed. Countries like Moldova offer an almost bottomless supply of new, fresh and (above all) young 'meat' to be sold, used and re-used. Even if a nation as poor as Moldova could stem the endless flow of women across its distinctly leaky borders, there will always be somewhere else to take its place. In that regard, sex trafficking is no different to any other globalised business: just as clothing brands switch their manufacture from one country to the next in the constant search for lower costs, so do sex traffickers. But if that's the supply side (as economists call it), what about demand? Now that's where our journey resumes.

Remember those trafficked women we met in Moldova? Remember the countries they were sent to? Did you notice anything? All of them were rich and (to a greater or lesser degree) modern, industrialised economies. The people who live in those countries have disposable incomes on a scale that could only be dreamed of in places like Chişinău. They have money to spend on satisfying not just the basic necessities of life but 'luxuries' too.

Our journey from Moldova is about to take us all across those rich modern countries: we're taking a whistle-stop tour of Western Europe. But we're not sightseeing, for this is a journey into misery and cynical exploitation. And not just the sort of exploitation we've met before; this journey is about the way entire cities, sometimes whole countries, get fat on the profits of slavery.

La Jonquera was once a small, sleepy Catalonian village of pretty ochre-coloured houses nestled along the Spanish side of the border with France. Like any rural village, its 1,000 or so inhabitants largely depended on agriculture and livestock for a living, but in the 1990s commerce came to La Jonquera. First, it was cross-border consumer traffic – cigarettes in Spain are around half the price of the same brands on sale in France; alcohol and petrol were also significantly cheaper. This cut-price shopping acted as 'pull factor', drawing thousands of visitors across the border every year.

La Jonquera found itself at the epicentre of a mini

economic boom. The town doubled in size as commercial traffic doubled in volume. Today, this once inconspicuous little place boasts 16 supermarkets, 16 petrol stations, 46 restaurants and more than 400 shops. But it has also been invaded by a very different sort of business: sex.

Prostitution isn't legal in Spain. It's not illegal, either: the government simply turns a blind eye to the selling of human bodies for 'recreation'. The result is that almost every town and sizeable village has a brothel and the difference between them and La Jonquera is simply one of scale.

It's hard to miss Club Paradise. A vast two-tone brown structure, conveniently situated behind a 24-hour petrol station, come dusk its huge illuminated signs flare out over the town, proclaiming it to be a 'nightclub' with 'showgirls'. In fact, Club Paradise is Europe's biggest brothel. And that's official.

It cost more than €3 million to build and inside its 27,000 square metres 1,800 women work 24 hours a day, seven days a week, servicing the demands of men for sex. And the men come – from other parts of Spain, from France and now on organised international tour groups.

Stop for a moment and think about that: 1,800 women selling their bodies in a town with a total population of less than 2,700 people. Yes, 1,800 women. Maybe you're reading this in a small town or village: try and imagine that same scenario in your own community. Wouldn't you want to know how it could happen? And wouldn't you want to know where all the women came from, and how they ended up where you live?

The man who owns and runs Club Paradise is called José Moreno; he runs two other brothels in two other towns in Spain. When he announced plans to build his mega-brothel in La Jonquera, the local mayor refused to grant him a licence because police had indicated Moreno was involved in international sex trafficking, but he sued and in 2010, the Supreme Court of Catalonia ruled that 'police speculation' was insufficient grounds to prevent the club from opening for business.

Many other businesses in the town were quite happy to welcome Mr Moreno's brothel, though. Since it opened two years ago, the trade in food, petrol and other consumer purchases has steadily gone up. So, what's the problem?

Firstly there's that police speculation. Except that it's no longer speculation. In 2012, Moreno was charged and convicted of international sex trafficking; of luring women – primarily from Brazil – to work as prostitutes in his clubs.[1] He was sentenced to three years in prison.

And then there were the women themselves. Where do you think all the prostitutes working round the clock in Club Paradise come from? Not from Spain, that's for sure. In fact, less than 2 per cent of Spain's estimated 300,000 prostitutes are Spanish; the vast majority come from Eastern Europe and, apparently, from Romania in particular. Of course they are not all Romanian. The relatively few police raids that have taken place in Spain have shown that many are from Moldova, and have either travelled on dual-nationality passports[2] or they have been given bogus Romanian documents. Either way, they end up selling their bodies in Spain – and not just in mega-brothels like Club Paradise.

It's one of the most depressing sights to come across in broad daylight. On a roundabout in the middle of La Jonquera, dozens of young women totter unsteadily on high heels, clothed in skimpy and skintight Lycra. Dozens more line the many overnight truck stops on the edge of town. These women – though really no more than teenage girls – are also 'Romanian'. They sell their bodies for a fraction of the price of those in Club Paradise: the going rate for oral sex can be as low as €5, with full intercourse from as little as €10.

Those who defend Spain's 'tolerant' attitude to prostitution like to claim that these women are economic migrants: they have a commodity in demand in the West and can earn comparative fortunes here by voluntarily selling sex. The problem with that is that no one actually knows whether all these teenagers have, voluntarily and on their own, travelled several thousand miles to a country they don't know to prostitute themselves to men whose languages they can't understand. Only occasionally do any facts emerge. And when they do, it doesn't look pretty.

Valentina arrived in La Jonquera one night in April 2011. Back home in Moldova, she had met a man who wanted to be her boyfriend. After a few days of seeing each other, he told her that he could get a well-paid job working in a hotel in Spain. Valentina was torn: she had young children and would have to leave them in the care of her family but there was no chance of earning good money in

Moldova and besides, her new boyfriend was going to come with her.

You can guess the rest, can't you?

They crossed the border into Romania and obtained perfectly legal EU travel documents, but when they got to Spain, Valentina's boyfriend told her she was not going to work in a hotel: instead they stopped at the roundabout and he forced her out of the car. When she refused, he threatened first to beat her and then to have her children back in Moldova killed.

And so for two weeks Valentina endured dozens of men abusing her body: in cars, in trucks, on the rough, hard ground next to the road. She earned a little over €2,000 in that short time and all of it handed over to her 'boyfriend'. One day she made a plan to escape; she managed to hitch a lift to the local police station and tried to tell them her story but the police simply shrugged their shoulders. According to them it was a crime out of their jurisdiction and she would have to go to the regional police bureau, 15 kilometres away, they said. Valentina had no chance of getting that far away so she returned to the roundabout. A few days later, she disappeared. No one knows what happened to her.

Does this make you angry? I hope so, because in every Valentina, in every trafficked and abused woman, I see myself. I see myself in Amsterdam, being pawed and penetrated by carefree men with money to spend but no conscience as to how they spent it. And it makes me angry that this hasn't stopped. On the contrary, it's getting worse.

Spain has now become a country rapidly modelling part

of its economy on Amsterdam's model. Package sex holidays are a new form of industry and in a country where the economy is hanging on by a thread, the government isn't about to turn away any business, even if that involves the trafficking of sex slaves. Even conservative estimates put the amount of money involved at €40 billion a year – the same figure as Spain spends on schools and education.

Just about the only real attempt at any constant policing is run by the brothel owners themselves. A few of them formed a self-regulating trade body known as the Asociación Nacional de Empresarios de Locales de Alterne (ANELA).[3] As a condition of membership, a club must be a properly registered business, such as a hotel or bar licensed for renting rooms. It must also expressly undertake not to allow anyone under 18 on the premises, any use of drugs or involuntary prostitution. Furthermore, the club must agree to co-operate fully with the police, while ensuring monthly medical checks-up for the women.

But ANELA represents just 200 of the estimated 4,000 brothels littered across Spain. Many of the remainder are controlled by criminal gangs, who have trafficked women from poorer countries with the promise of conventional work. Deprived of their passports and physically intimidated, these women are forced to work as prostitutes while earning their bosses vast profits. They are slaves, just as Valentina was… and just as I was.

These criminal networks shift and change shape constantly, in tune with the global market place. Some are one- or two-man operations – much as the one run by the man who trafficked me from England, except that these are based in Moldova and Romania. Others, though, are true global businesses, operated by established organised crime groups in Nigeria or China.

Deputy Inspector Xavier Cortés Camacho is the head of Spain's regional anti-trafficking unit in Barcelona. His team's investigations revealed how the Nigerian groups trafficked their victims across Northern Africa to Spain – and then controlled them by threatening to rape or kill their family members back home. But in a globalised economy, where money speaks louder than the pain of slavery, Cortés Camacho and his officers fight a losing battle. How can they keep up with such a profitable and international black market, operated by traffickers from at least a dozen countries? He knows the answer: they can't. Because even though the Spanish government estimates that more than 90 per cent of the prostitutes working there have been trafficked, no one cares enough about these women – women whose bodies are broken to make men profits – to put a stop to the practice.

It's a measure of how far the traffickers are ahead of anti-trafficking efforts that until recently, police in Barcelona did not even realise that Chinese mafias ran prostitution rings in the city. They then began to notice more and more advertisements for Chinese, Japanese and Korean women – all of them, it turned out, Chinese – working in a network of about 30 brothels. The working conditions were brutal. Mr Cortés and his team installed electronic bugs in some of these brothels and heard the women complain that they were in pain or they needed rest. But their slave masters ignored such pleas and instead made them service yet more men. One of these young Chinese slaves discovered she had contracted HIV. She committed suicide – and there was still nothing the police could do.

And it's not just Spain. Every country in Western Europe has a vast population of prostitutes: every single one.

Is this a new phenomenon? No, of course it's not (though it is a growing one). There has always been prostitution and there probably always will be so long as men view women as commodities they can buy and sell. But look a little closer with me and you'll see something revealing.

There are 27 countries in the European Union. Only six of them – Austria, Germany, Greece, Hungary, Latvia and Holland – have actively legalised prostitution and allow brothels to be set up as normal commercial businesses.[4] The other 21 countries either outlaw the whole thing or like Spain, settle for a haphazard approach which technically permits women to accept money for sex, but criminalises anyone who helps them to do so.

And here's the funny thing. When I started out on this journey, I was told that legalising prostitution reduces sex trafficking. In which case those countries who have gone the whole hog and torn up the law book should have the smallest problem; countries like Spain and Britain, who operate a policy of quasi-legal tolerance should have more women sold into sex slavery, and the countries who make any form of paying for sex illegal should have the biggest problem with trafficking. What I discovered is that the truth is the exact opposite.

Why should this be? It's as simple and as scientific as all successful commodity trading. Demand – the pull factor in economic equations – goes up when men can abuse women's bodies without fear of prosecution. This creates a market, which businesses – or crime gangs – service with the cheapest 'commodities' they can lay their hands on. It means trafficked women, because sex slaves don't get any wages, don't have any employment rights and come from countries that are desperately poor and unable to support them (what's known in market economics as 'the push factor'). Everywhere I looked across Europe the stories of individual women – ordinary women like you and like I once was – painted the same picture. We have become just another global commodity to be bought, sold and subsequently discarded.

Do you know the value of a human life? Of course that's a loaded question: economists will tell you that a life in, say, rural Moldova has less financial worth than one in London or Barcelona, or Amsterdam. But sex-traffickers are not concerned with the nuances of macro-economics; they work to a very accurate business plan and thanks to studies of their operations across Europe we now know the price of a life: €67,200. On average, that's what a trafficked sex slave earns per year in an industrialised country for the man who owns her.

Does that sound brutal and calculating? I hope it revolts and repulses you. But that's how the men who trade in human flesh run their businesses and measure their success.

Do you remember where we started this chapter – with

the invention of the barcode? Over the past 40 years it has quietly revolutionised international commerce, applying science to the buying and selling of goods the world over. How long do you think it will be before sex traffickers adopt it – five years, ten years? Well, think again. Because they already have.

In March 2012, Spanish police broke up an international prostitution business based in Madrid. They raided a series of brothels owned by a consortium of 22 Romanian men from two rival gangs: inside they found women who had been held against their will, chained to radiators, beaten and whipped. Their hair and eyebrows had been shaved off if they refused to work as sex slaves. The police also found guns, ammunition, gold and €140,000 in cash, hidden behind a false ceiling.

But what else did they discover? They discovered barcodes tattooed on the womens' wrists. Each code contained the name of her owner and the amount she had cost him to purchase from other traffickers.

Have you heard enough yet? Are you still with me? Because there's one more place I have to go and it will take all the strength and courage I have left: I have to return to Hell. Will you come with me?

---

[1] At the time of writing, Moreno was challenging that conviction in the Spanish courts.

[2] Two-thirds of Moldovans have the right to Romanian citizenship. This is a major problem for EU countries since Romania is a

member of the European Union and its citizens have the right to travel freely throughout it, whereas Moldova is not.

[3] In Spain, brothels are known as 'Clubes de Alterne' – literally translated, this means socialising clubs.

[4] Switzerland and Turkey, both in Europe but not members of the EU, have also legalised prostitution.

CHAPTER SEVEN

1012

One and a half acres, 20 streets, 142 brothels, more than 300 'windows', at least 8,000 prostitutes... Welcome to Dutch Postcode 1012: Amsterdam's Red Light District. Welcome to Hell.

We have been here before, you and I. Here, you watched me sold into slavery; here, you saw men abuse my body for their brutal 15 minutes of lust; here, you wept – I hope – as I ceased to be Sarah Forsyth and became a 'prosty', a ravaged and hopeless crack whore. And now we're back.

We have come to tell a new story that is, at the same time, the same as the old one. We've come to see what – if anything – has changed in this cleverly organised place of despair since my ordeal here, more than 15 years ago. In these old streets we will find pain and torture, callousness and indifference, but we will also find love and hope and the first glimmerings of a terrible realisation. We are to meet people here, you and I: each has his own story that, together, will make up the picture of this place. But for this picture to mean anything, you must be part of it – as must I. Are you strong enough – am *I* strong enough? This journey will take all my newfound strength: are you ready to make it with me?

But where shall we start? And how? With a photo – *that* photo, which started this book – and with flowers. The photo belongs to Amsterdam just as surely as I once did; it will dog our every step through this city, always in our minds as we meet and listen to each new story. But first...

It is spring. The Netherlands is in bloom, its daffodils and tulips everywhere. In Amsterdam the city's flower market is crowded by day as thousands of tourists mingle with local people, all buying the pretty blooms to decorate their homes.

But now it is evening. On the third floor of an old and slightly dishevelled building on the edge of the Red Light District a tall and beautiful blonde woman in her mid-40s is working quietly with a group of young men and women. They are carefully placing flowers and an individual chocolate egg into small hand-baskets, each no bigger than a paperback book. There are more than 300 of these little baskets: one for each of the neon-lit windows in the surrounding streets. The tall blonde woman is Toos Heemskirk and she has a big part to play in this story.

A hundred miles away, in a quiet provincial town in the middle of the Netherlands, a solemn, balding man sits at a desk in his modern, air-conditioned office. He is looking at those photos and with them reports from Dutch police intelligence. His name is Werner ten Kate, and he too will be important for us to meet.

Our picture cuts back to Amsterdam. Halfway down an anonymous street, two miles from the city centre but still running beside one of its trademark canals, a group of young women noisily prepare a sizeable evening meal. They speak different languages, these women, and are from half a dozen different countries, yet they work together cheerfully, as a vast pot of rice boils on the stove. However diverse their backgrounds, they all have one thing in common. We shall return here to listen to their stories.

And what of the Red Light District itself, this lovely April evening? The windows are now lit up, each holding a woman in a tiny bikini, who alternately beckons to the passing crowds or sits listlessly on a stool, smoking cigarette after cigarette. In the streets around, on corners or seeming to hug the growing shadows, are young men wearing leather jackets. Their gaze, unlike so many of the women they guard, is sharp and vigilante as they scan the bustle of tourists. Two uniformed policemen on pushbikes ride past them; neither acknowledges the other. De Rosse Burt – as the Dutch know this place – is ready for another night of industrialised sex.

At its lower edge, people are slowly straggling into the 14th-century *Oude Kirk*, or 'Old Church'. It is almost Easter, and there are still those who choose the house of God over the pleasures of the flesh.

Toos Heemskirk is one of those – though to meet her

you'd never know. She is not overtly religious, never once pressing her faith on anyone else. But for 15 years, she has quietly walked the streets of the Red Light District, with love. She and a handful of other volunteers are members of Scharlaken Koord – The Scarlet Cord (http://wellspringinternational.org/projects/scarlet-cord/) – a Christian organisation which visits the women in the neon-lit windows, offering them friendship, medical help and the promise that if they ever want to get out of prostitution, Scharlaken Koord will help them.[1]

This evening, Toos and her young friends will take the little baskets of flowers and offer one to each of the women working in the Red Light District. Toos says: 'It is Easter so we are going to give out flowers and give them an Easter greeting with some chocolate. Dutch flowers, donated by persons to give out, so it's nice for these women – it touches their heart because the majority of the tourists see them just as a piece of meat. They just gaze at women, or maybe they go in and use her for sex.

'But we go to them and just give a flower. We hope to let them feel that they are worthwhile, much more than a piece of meat: they are persons, they are women. We know this may seem such a small thing, but it is meaningful for these women. We are going to give out 300, but we might not have enough even with that number.'

As they walk down the narrow alleyways, the volunteers stop at every window. They knock politely on the glass. Some of the women open the door, smile briefly and accept the flowers before quickly – very quickly – resuming their mannequin-like pose. Others shake their heads or ignore the offer, furtively glancing at the leather-jacketed men lurking nearby. Only a handful speak to Toos and her friends. Undeterred, they move on through the crowds of tourists, pimps and customers. Throughout the evening there is an underlying tension, a sense of violence waiting to happen. Toos explained: 'It is not pleasant because tonight there have been some clients and they wanted to bargain with the price: they saw the price was €50 and they wanted to start with €30. And they were kind of, you know, aggressive, which was very uncomfortable for the women. But that is how it is, here. Always.'

I wish Toos had been in these streets when I was here. She is warm and caring, and I know how much that would have meant to me when I was trapped behind the glass windows she visits. But her work is not just pastoral: it enables Toos and her helpers to collect vital information on the ground intelligence about the reality of the Red Light District, and especially how this has changed in the years since I was here. 'The biggest change is because of the European Union. Over the last 10 years or so, after the end of the Iron Curtain and the expansion of the EU, what I have seen happening is a huge number of women coming here from Eastern Europe. We have girls from Albania, the Czech Republic, Bulgaria, Romania and Russia. At the same time, Holland has legalised prostitution and this has meant that more and more girls come here to work in the windows.'

To walk with Toos through the Red Light District is to take a tour not just through human misery but one in which the selling of womens' bodies is a microcosm of global commerce. Toos explains: 'Cheap goods flow out of their impoverished source countries and into rich Western nations, with the money to buy – or at least rent – them. There are different streets in the Red Light District, different zones, which are used by different nationalities. There is a street where the majority are Hungarian girls from one small town: they actually call this the Neregaze Street because that is the place in Northeast Hungary where those girls are coming from. Then you have another street on the other side where the majority of the women are Bulgarian. And then this area where we are walking now, the majority of the girls are from the Dominican Republic. Occasionally you find Hungarian and Bulgarian girls next to each other, but mostly they are placed together by the brothel owners, who come from those places themselves.'

Toos walks along the Voorburgwal Canal, its limpid and sluggish water reflecting the constant glow of neon from the other side of the street, then turns into the small and fetid lanes of Trompettersteeg and Goldbergsteed. On the corner is a window I once knew well. This was the glass box in which I was imprisoned and forced to allow my body to be raped, and raped again.

It was the place where I first forged a relationship with Sally, the English girl who had helped lure me into an existence – not a life – of sex slavery. Behind that glass I had sucked greedily on my first joint; in the grubby area behind was where I first tasted crack cocaine and began to imprison myself behind its walls of addiction.

It looked exactly the same.

There was a girl in the window: a girl with short dark hair and olive-coloured skin. The tiny strips of fabric barely covered her pitifully thin frame. She looked to be in her 20s, her late 20s. But somehow, I knew she was younger. Who was she? Where was she from?

But there was no chance to find out. Toos warned that the men in leather jackets were watching, circling. It would not be safe to approach this girl: these men were the 'running boys', who kept a constant eye on 'their' windows. Not, of course, that they owned or even rented them: they simply worked for a pimp who controlled that sector of Hell. Toos said: 'I know this street: whenever I would take something to the window you will see, all of a sudden there will be men around me. And they keep a special eye, they are attentive; they are out there. Of course, the big guys, the pimps themselves, they are not in the street – they have these other persons, these running boys, looking out.

'This area is for the Hungarians, and the Hungarian pimps they bring their cousins, they bring their family members to work as their eyes and ears. They are out in the cafés to kind of protect their merchandise. It is like a Mafia.'

Nothing had changed. The girl in the window might have been from Eastern Europe, not Northeast England, but the same vicious criminals kept her there, and the same heedless herds of tourist cattle either gawped at her emaciated body or paid €50 to abuse it. Nothing, nothing, had really changed.

It should have; it was meant to have changed. Five years

after I was trafficked here, four years after I escaped from this cesspit, the Dutch government changed the law. When I was here, prostitution was neither legal nor illegal – it just 'happened' and the authorities turned a blind eye, even if that meant ignoring the women like me who were tricked into prostitution then trapped behind the glass by violent pimps.

In 2000, all that was supposed to change. A new law was brought in to make prostitution legal: any woman over the age of 18 and holding a European Union passport who wanted to sell her body was allowed to set herself up in business, to rent a room in which to work and to open a bank account – just like any other self-employed trader. She could even, if she wanted to, work for an 'employer', or pimp.

To make all of this even easier, the laws which outlawed brothels and pimps were also repealed: existing brothels – including the Red Light District windows – were given a licence by the local City Council. In return, the owner of the building had to install panic buttons in every room used for prostitution, and to provide condoms.

Local police would patrol Red Light District areas to keep a careful eye on this legal and licensed selling of sex. The idea was that if individual women were allowed to sell sex without fear of arrest then somehow sex trafficking and the criminal gangs who bought and sold womens' unwilling bodies across international borders would magically disappear.

Less than a mile away from the heart of the Red Light District, a warm, open and handsome man, wearing a startlingly blue open-necked shirt, sits in a quiet garden.

Harold van Gelder is the head of Amsterdam's anti-trafficking detective squad. Van Gelder told us: 'You know, the Dutch legislators have not lost their mind in prostitution policy; there is a vision behind it. One of the positive advantages of our policy is that the prostitute has no fear of the police. It is a legal profession – if you follow the rules, the police won't bother you. Compare it to an iceberg, where you only see the tip of it – and I understand that we only see the tip of the iceberg – but at least it's a percentage of the branch we can control.

'You must understand we have experienced for 700 years in this area that there is prostitution. It is situated in the oldest part of Amsterdam and that can be explained by history. Where the central station is, there used to be a big port and where the ships came from the sea, and the sailors came off and they came into town and what were they looking for: booze and women. So it's quite familiar to the people who live in here. And during the centuries we have tried everything: for example, we've tried to ban prostitution from the streets of Amsterdam and that didn't stop it, so now we have the situation we have now where we try to control it with a legalised branch with permits.

'One of the objectives of legalisation is to build a form of relationship between a policeman and the women, by being there if they have any problems: in the end they can trust you as a policeman if they want to step forward and get out of the prostitution. You can compare it to domestic violence: why does a woman stay at home if she is being beaten every week? Because of her children, because of the money – but in the end she says enough is enough.

'It's the same with prostitution – there is always a relationship between the prostitute and her pimp or trafficker. It could be a love relation, or a business relation or fearful relation. She has to come to the point where she is willing to get help and trust the police. In a lot of countries the police are not your best friend. Here, we have to earn their trust.'

So how does it work, this earning of trust? For a start, all police officers working for the anti-trafficking squad are hand-picked: each has to undertake an additional 256 hours of specialised training in how to speak to – to interview, in police-speak – a suspected victim of sex slavery.

'So it is not all the policemen who do the controlling; they have been appointed, and they have been given extra tools and training. We try to visit each brothel, window, club or massage parlour six times a year at least. And our officers always work under a code of conduct: for instance they work in pairs, we are not allowed to use any drinks or beverage when we enter these brothels and we always keep sight of each other because we don't want to split the teams within the brothel because there is the risk of corruption, of course.

'Inside a brothel we look for three things. We mainly focus on minors: no one is allowed to work in prostitution under 18 years of age. Second of all, you have to be legal to work here in Holland, and third, we don't want any people forced to be working in prostitution by trafficking. But it is really hard for a policeman to find out from an interview of 10 to 15 minutes if someone is forced but we try to pick up little signals, things that make us think there is something going on.

'For instance if the police officer enters the brothel and asks the lady that is working there for her identity papers, and she says that she has to make a phone call to ask their boyfriend to bring her documents, for me as a police officer that is a signal of trafficking. If she doesn't have her passport, why is that?

'Another signal is that she is afraid of the police, afraid to be expelled from the country or afraid of the boyfriend who is standing outside and is obviously worried why these police are staying so long. So there are tiny things we try to pick up and start an investigation on that.'

Harold van Gelder is a good man. He devotes his working day (and many nights) to helping women who – just as I was – are beaten and threatened into selling their bodies. And he cares, he cares deeply. But Harold has a team of just seven detectives: seven men and women to 'control' more than 300 brothels and 'interview' at least 8,000 prostitutes. How effective can he possibly be? And did you notice that little phrase 'at least 8,000 prostitutes'? It may come as a surprise, but no one – not the Dutch government, not Amsterdam City Council, not even Harold van Gelder – knows how many women are working in the sex trade, let alone how many of them have been trafficked and forced into it.

'No, it is not possible. We don't even know how many prostitutes are working in Amsterdam because we do not register prostitutes. If she is over 18, if she is doing this voluntarily – at least if she is saying so – and she is

147

allowed to work here, why should the police register them? We don't register all the butchers and the bakers in Amsterdam.

'To our law it is a normal profession. If the owners of the premises uphold the conditions of their permit, they are allowed to exploit prostitution business there. As police, we try to control them, to check the womens' identity and so on, but if everything is OK, why should we register them?'

As I say, Harold van Gelder is a good, decent man. And he does a good, decent job. But do you think being pawed and penetrated, bought and used, a dozen or more times a day is a 'normal profession'? Do you think it's the same as being a baker or a butcher? I've been in those windows, I've endured the brutal thrust and grind of selfish men who had enough spare cash to rent my mouth and my vagina. It might have some connection with butchery and meat, I suppose, but it's nothing – absolutely nothing – like baking bread. I promise you.

Of course, Harold's team aren't the only police officers who 'control' the Red Light District. Do you remember the uniformed officers on bicycles we saw, speeding past the pimps' running boys earlier? Look, says Amsterdam, we have bobbies on bikes patrolling these streets.

I remember those police. I remember the ones who raped me – seven of them – because they knew my owner and he had given them 'a freebie': a gift of my body to do with as they pleased, even though I told them I didn't want to. How much do you think that has changed? Let's ask another woman – a Dutch woman – who worked the windows. She has no axe to grind for she is one of the few, the very few, who had the 'freedom' to choose her job.

Patricia Perquin worked as a prostitute in Amsterdam for over four years. She had huge debts as a result of her 'addiction' to shopping and was staring bankruptcy in its unforgiving face. A friend suggested she should go into prostitution to pay her debts off. Never, she told herself. Three weeks later, as panic and desperation took hold, she was selling her body in one of the Red Light District windows.

She is frank about the effect it had on her – and the dangers involved.

> You cannot imagine what it's like to be a prostitute. If you let down your guard for a minute or even a second, you could pay with your life in the Red Light District. No one wants to play Russian roulette, watching your back and looking round just in time to make sure no one is about to strangle you. No one wants to undergo the humiliation I have experienced. And I probably got off lightly, if I compare my experiences with other prostitutes.

But what Patricia Perquin really wants you to know is the reality – the sordid, banal reality – behind the cosy notion that policing in the Red Light District is effective. Because in her experience the very people who are supposed to make sure these women are working legally and have not been coerced into prostitution are still on remarkably friendly terms with the pimps.

As a woman in the windows, you see the police drinking coffee with your landlord one minute and with you the next minute. Then you see them helping out with tours of the area organised by commercial companies. How are you supposed to build up a relationship of trust? Whose side are they on?

What do you think? I know – for every good, honest cop like Harold van Gelder and his dedicated team, somewhere there is always one who is taking a kickback. It might be cash – and we'll come to the huge mountain of cash in a minute – or it might be 'freebies'.

There's an old phrase about this situation, one my gran likes and still uses: 'He's either a knave or a fool'. Amsterdam's anti-trafficking squad doesn't fall into either category but someone, somewhere, in the Dutch government or police is either blind as a bat or deliberately not seeing what's in front of them.

How do I know, you say? Is all of this coloured – indelibly stained – by what happened to me? Maybe things have really got better, and perhaps I just don't want to see it? I wish you were right – I wish, I really wish, that were true.

I'm not particularly well educated; I never went to university and got a degree, but even I know the simple principle that college people called Occam's Razor. Put bluntly, it says that when faced with a situation that needs unpicking, the simple explanation is better than a more complicated one. Or, as we tend to put it where I come from: 'If it looks like a duck, quacks like a duck – guess what it is?'

So let's start with that in mind and look at Amsterdam's

Red Light District today, shall we? Fact: there are at least 8,000 prostitutes working there and despite what Harold van Gelder says, that's an official Dutch government estimate. That same official source says that the vast majority, at least 80 per cent, come from foreign countries: Hungary, Romania, Moldova, Slovakia, the Balkans and Africa.

Now the complicated explanation for this is that each of these women – most of whom don't speak a word of English (a pretty much universal language in the Netherlands), let alone Dutch – paid for their travel to Amsterdam, then located – with no help – the correct government department to present their passport, got it stamped and then went out and negotiated rents not just for a flat but for a place to sell sex. All off her own bat.

The simple 'it's a duck' principle says: someone brought this woman to Amsterdam, sorted out all the paperwork and then made her work as a prostitute to pay back this 'debt'. Which one do you think is the more likely? Toos Heemskirk knows – and she has been up and down these streets for 15 years. 'I have been working here since 1995. And now? I mean, how can a girl from Albania out of a village – I don't know where from – know her way to Amsterdam? Know where to live, how to rent a window? There must be an organised crime behind it. I mean, we have to be looking at a mafia-type organisation.'

Still undecided? Still not quite ready to believe that Amsterdam – lovely, quaint old Amsterdam, with its canals and tulips and its Anne Frank house for tourists who actually care to find out about young girls under the threat of death – could allow organised crime to run its most famous streets?

Still think that the Yugoslav criminals who beat me, drugged me and made me watch a bewildered new 'prosty' being shot to death as part of a snuff film have been magicked away by a whole new breed of happy, willing hookers? Come and meet Jerrol Martens. He can tell you the truth – it's his job.

He's a big man is Jerrol – big in the same physical way as Ion Vizdoga: strong, calm and yet passionate. Jerrol runs CoMensha, the Netherland's national trafficking reporting organisation. And he – unlike Harold van Gelder – has a very clear idea of the numbers of women forced into the country's legalised prostitution industry.

'If you look at the figures from last year [2010], we had 1,000 registered victims of human trafficking: about 80 per cent were sent into the sex industry. But to be honest, I think this is just the tip of the iceberg. Prostitution here used to be dominated by Dutch women, who for a large part worked voluntarily, of their own will. But because of the demand mainly for younger women, for the past 10 to 15 years this has changed and we now see that prostitutes here are mainly from Africa and Eastern Europe. What's more, the information we get from women that have been freed from this situation is that a lot of times they have been forced in coming to Holland. For instance, if you take the Nigerian girls they are bonded by voodoo rituals; they are too scared to leave because they are being threatened they will die, or their families will be victims.

'From the Eastern European girls it is more abusive; that

they will be abused before they leave, beat them up or threaten that if they don't work as prostitutes their traffickers will harm their families. So, they are being beaten into a situation to leave their own country and a lot of times during the travel from Eastern Europe to Holland they are being abused, they are being raped – it is really very violent.

'Then when the women finally get here their traffickers take away the passports and papers. They say: "We've paid your way over here so you have to pay back, you have to pay for the room, you have to pay for the condoms, you have to pay for everything, for the food – and so you must work for us for no money."

'As a result most of the time the women never get out of the place they stay. They are being brought to the rooms that they work in and they are brought back to where they sleep. The traffickers and pimps keep them sheltered from the outside world. These girls don't speak the language, they don't know where they are, and they don't know anything of their surroundings except going to work, back and forth, and sleeping. Mostly, they have a low IQ. From the victims that we've found it is often very hard for them to be returned back home because they don't actually know where they are from, or how they got into this situation.'

Tell me, does this sound familiar? Jerrol Martens was exactly describing that spring in 2011 – and I mean, word for word – what had happened to me 15 years earlier. The only real difference between then and now is that I was trafficked from England whereas today's victims are imported from much cheaper sources: capitalism at its finest. But wasn't it to stop this international trade in human flesh and misery that the Netherland's made prostitution, pimps and brothel-keeping legal? Wasn't the whole idea to take commercial sex out of the hands of criminals? We shall shortly see, you and I, how this well-intentioned theory has worked in practice, but first we need to meet Karina Schaapman.

Karina has been many things in her life. A poverty-stricken only child, she grew up in the southern Dutch city of Leiden, 40 kilometres from Amsterdam. Her father walked out on the day Karina was born, and she grew up in a tiny flat with her mother. Money was either tight or non-existent: most weeks the cash ran out early and both mother and daughter knew the meaning of true, crippling hunger. But when Karina was 13 her mother was struck down with bouts of vicious stomach pain. A year later, she was dead and Karina was sent to live with the father she had never met. He turned out to be rather free with his fists, and unwilling to bear his abuse, she ran away to Amsterdam. There she found somewhere to stay, surrounded by the bars and brothels of the city. What happened next was wearily inevitable: unable to support herself any other way, she was forced to sell her body in the Red Light District.

Karina's history struck a chord with me. Although not identical, our childhoods had striking similarities: an abusive father, a devoted mother, chronic poverty, we could have been sisters. But it is what Karina did next that makes her so vital to our story. She got herself out prostitution, raised her own family and then became a politician. Not just any politician: she got herself elected to Amsterdam City Council, with responsibility for education. But her past was about to come back to haunt her.

One day, in the playground of her children's school, another pupil's father accosted her: he knew her from her previous life as a prostitute. She realised that it would be only a matter of time before the news of her former existence leaked out, but instead of quietly trying to hide it, Karina outed herself, writing a book about her experiences. And instead of this damaging her, the Dutch public supported her: as a result Karina was able to speak out about the reality of prostitution in the city.

Together with another member of the council, she put together an investigative dossier on the way women were trafficked into the Red Light District and what happened to them there. As the two women presented the report, tellingly titled 'Making the Visible Invisible', Karina bluntly announced: 'There are people who are really proud of the Red Light District as a tourist attraction. It's supposed to be a wonderful relaxed place that shows just what a free city we are, but I think it's a cesspit. There's a lot of serious criminality, there's a lot of exploitation of women and a lot of social distress – that's nothing to be proud of.'

And what was it – above all else – that Karina Schaapman's dossier showed? That the majority – the vast majority – of the 8,000 women working in the windows, the brothels and the clubs of Amsterdam had been forced to do so by violent pimps and traffickers. Worse still, there was a whole other group of prostitutes selling their bodies in Amsterdam that no one – not even the police or the Council – knew anything about, much less monitored. These women were selling their bodies via internet-based 'escort services' which didn't fall under any of the licensing regulations brought in between 2000 and 2008. No one knew who they were, where they came from or whether they were working willingly, but the clues were there.

Karina explained: 'There is no way to get a true picture of what is going on, but if in a newspaper a girl is on offer for €50 for an entire night, to be picked up in Amsterdam-West, you know something has to be very wrong.

And what do you think happened next? Did Amsterdam rise up and support this brave woman, fighting to protect young girls who, just as she herself had been, were used and abused? No, it was quite the opposite.

'In particular, Mariska Majoor, a former prostitute who runs an information centre at De Wallen, rose up in arms. We were was supposedly exaggerating: no more than 20 per cent were working involuntarily behind the windows. I have no idea where she got that figure but still, even if one in five prostitutes was forced into it that seems to me a sufficient number to talk about huge abuse.

'At the same time, a lobby of Red Light District promoters has risen, guided by Mariska Majoor. She blames me for smearing prostitution, just because I myself have had negative experiences. It is just unbelievable what kind of resistance this issue evokes. Even with women, particularly with women. If you fight prostitution, you often hear the claim that the amount of rapes will increase. Er, hello! Saying something like that means you would sacrifice other women just for your own security.

'There is no public indignation over the oppression of these women. This is partly due to ignorance, but there is also a sense that "it is the way it is". We cannot allow that.'

No, we can't. But we do.

It is evening again. We must cross Amsterdam's busy streets, filled with cyclists and trams. We must go back to that warm kitchen in the anonymous house near the canal, where girls from a bewildering variety of countries are preparing an evening meal.

Susanna is tiny. I'm not tall – a little over five feet on a good day and in decent shoes – and my weight has stabilised to the average for an English girl of my size (around seven-and-a-half stone). But Susanna is even shorter and thinner than I am. Her eyes are dark, with heavy circles underneath: they are also red-rimmed from crying.

Sitting next to her on one of those brightly coloured sofas that you see in places like IKEA is another waif-like girl. Her name is Mardea: in her native country of Sierra Leone it means 'first-born girl'. As she speaks, she grips and twists a paper tissue between her fingers.

Mardea and Susanna arrived in this warm, friendly house three days ago. It is a shelter for women who have been trafficked into Amsterdam's sex industry. We need to listen to these women, you and me: we need to hear their stories to understand the reality of the Red Light District today. We need to know who the girls behind the famous glass windows are. Let's start with Susanna.

I am from Hungary. Until last year I lived with my mum in Budapest. One day I left our flat to go to buy some cigarettes for my mum at the petrol station.

A man came up to me there and offered to sell me some. I was about to tell him no when he put a handkerchief over my mouth and I don't know how but I somehow fell asleep.

When I awoke, I was in a flat with this man. He made me have sex with him. He raped me. Three times he did it to me. And he beat me, very badly. He punched me in the face two times and then he was strangling me and saying that I had to work for him and if I did not agree he would kill me. I was so scared and so I agreed: I had no choice.

He gave me a drink and a cigarette and I began to feel very strange – dizzy and sleepy. I can remember him and another man putting me into a car and then – it seemed like just the next minute – we were at the airport in Budapest. I could not speak very well but the man who had raped me told me we were going to another country, where I would work for him. He had got my passport from my handbag, where I always kept it. In Hungary it is good to keep your passport with you because if you are stopped by police or something you can identify yourself.

We got on the plane and I fell asleep; I felt so strange and like I was in a dream. When we got off the plane, I did not know where I was. The man made a phone call and I could hear him telling the person at the other end that I would arrive somewhere at one o'clock. That was in the next morning.

He took me to a building and upstairs into a flat. There was another man there and I was handed over to him. Then this man from Budapest left. I was so tired that I wanted just to have a shower and go to bed. But the new man told me I could not. He made me sit in the living room and then he forced me to have sex with him. I didn't want to and said, 'Why are you doing this to me?' but he kicked me in my side and said if I did not do what he told me the next time he would kick me in my head.

When he had finished he pushed me away and told me to sleep because I would soon be made to work. But I didn't dare to sleep: I was so afraid that I was awake all night.

In the morning the man took me to a place in the city. I didn't know which city it was, but there were girls behind glass windows and men were walking up and down the street. He pushed me inside one of the doors with the windows and there was another girl from Hungary. He told this girl to make sure I knew what to do.

I asked her: 'Where am I?' and she told me that I was in Amsterdam. She told me I was to work there in the room with the glass window from four in the afternoon until three in the next morning. I did not want to — I had never done anything like this in Hungary and it is shameful to me — but the girl said to me that the boss would come and kill me and her if I did not do this.

She told me I must have sex with 12 men every day. I told her I did not know what to do or what to say to men here because I speak only Hungarian. But she showed me a piece of paper with Hungarian words next to words in other languages. There was 'suck' and 'fuck' written on it and numbers — 35 and 50. Those were the prices.

The men came, one after one after one. It was so difficult for me, but I did not know what to do, and I was afraid of the boss man. Some of the men were from places where they spoke English — I know a very few English words — some others were Chinese.

The girl also gave me a mobile phone and told me that when a man had finished with me, I had to ring a telephone number to say he had left and how much he had paid. At the end of the working time she said a man would telephone me and ask me how much I earned and I was to tell him the correct numbers for the day and the night.

When the working time was over, I had €350. I was very afraid: I had not earned enough because I had not had sex with 12 men. The boss took the money from me and was angry. He said this was not enough because he had paid for me and also he had to pay rent for the place where I worked. He hit me in the face again and punched me in the stomach.

The next day I was taken to the glass window to work and I was very dizzy and not very awake. Then I felt that something was dripping from my nose to my legs and I looked and it was blood — I guess I had high blood pressure or something like that. But the man said I had to work.

Then a girl came to my working place and handed to me condoms. But the boss man told me I was not allowed to use them: he said if I didn't use a condom, I can earn more money.

I was working like this for many weeks. Every day, more men. It was very painful for me and I was very sad. It was terrible: I was forced to do things I didn't want to do. Really, it was so terrible. Every day I see the police going past the glass window, sometimes many times a day they would walk by or go along on bicycles, but I did not dare speak to them because I was afraid of the boss man; also he had my passport so I feared that if the police discovered me I would be put in prison for a long time. But the police never came to my working place to speak with me. Not one time.

Then one day – it was a Tuesday – one of the Hungarian girls helped me. I do not want to say her name because she is still here. She told the boss man that I was not well and that I needed to go to the hospital. He was angry and said I could not, but she was strong and told him I had to because I could not work.

At the hospital, I was shaking and in a very bad shape. The medical people there could see something was not right, so they first call for an interpreter and then they ask me for my story. I told them what happened to me and they brought me to this place: they told me it is a shelter for girls like me who have been made to do prostitution.

I am very happy to be here: I do not have to have sex with men any more like before. But I cannot sleep – I am afraid that the boss man will come for me and kill me, like he said. Even when I do fall asleep, I see his face in front of my eyes in my dreams and I wake up screaming. The other girls here do not like this, but they understand.

I am crying. I am the same age – exactly – as Susanna. I want to hold her and tell her she will be OK, that I too was once like this but that I have survived, that she will too. But I cannot. I may have escaped from this Hell, but

Susanna is still here, trapped in her mind by the shame of what happened to her, what her body was forced to endure. As she gets up to go back to the kitchen, she stops and says:

I want to go home. To Hungary. But how can I tell my mum what I have done?

The brightly coloured sofa now seems garish and out of place. How can something so cheerful be in this room, where a young girl has just poured out her misery? How can these happy colours exist in the same space as evil? But we are not finished yet, nowhere near.

Mardea shifts uncomfortably on the cushions. She speaks English well and has listened without any show of emotion to the translator as Susanna's story unfolded. Now it is her turn.

I am from Freetown. It is the capital city of Sierra Leone. Our country is in West Africa and it has a bad history. One of the reasons I am here, I think, is because of my childhood and my family. My father was a policeman but he was killed in the civil war in 1999. Our family house was burned down then and my mother disappeared. I do not know where she was taken or what has happened to her.

The rest of my family brought me up in a village outside the city but they are very traditional and wanted me to have female circumcision. This is a very terrible thing, very painful, and I did not want to do this so I ran away from my family to live in Freetown.

I am a Christian and I joined a small church in the place where I was. I told the church about the problems with my family and the people there said they would help me. One day there was a man at the church, a white man. He spoke English to me, but not well. He said that he could get me a better life if I was willing to do a voluntary job with the church in Ghana. I did not know where this country was, only that it was in Africa. But the man said that if I would go there and preach the word of God and help poor people there, it would be good for me.

I was excited and I said yes. I imagined great things: that my life was going to change and that I could maybe get education as well as work with the church. The man said he would get a passport for me and that I should meet him at the church in a few days' time. When that day came there was the man and two other white people, a husband and wife. They said we should all go to the airport now.

At the airport the lady went with me to the people – the police people – who look at passports. She had all my documents and explained to the police that we were travelling together. It was very fast and we got on the plane. I did not know how long it would take to get to Ghana but the journey seemed to take a long time.

When we arrived the place looked very different from my home country, but I did not know what Ghana looked like. The husband and the wife went away and the man from the church took me to a house by some water. I asked him, 'When I am going to the church and meet the other people who worship?' Then he told me there was no church, that this was not Ghana but that it was Europe. I began to argue but

163

he hit me and he told me that from this moment I belonged to him and I had to work for him.

I was very frightened and I asked him what this work was. He said, 'I will bring men and you must sleep with them. Your life will change, you will have lot of money.' I asked, 'You want me to be prostitute?' He said yes. I told him, 'No, I can't. This is not what you told me. You told me we were going to Ghana. Even if I had problems where I come from, I don't know this sort of life and I cannot do it.' But he hit me again and told me he had paid for my passport and visa, and that I owed him much money. He said I must have sex with men until this money was paid back.

I felt very bad. I was crying but I thought, if I fight, I am scared my life is at risk. No one would know if I was killed here. So I think I just said OK. I was just praying inside: 'God, this is not my wish. Please show me how to do this job but also, please help me to escape, to run out of this house.' Then the man locked me in the house on my own.

When he came back, he brought a man with him. He told me I was to let the man have sex with me. I was terrified: I had never slept with a white man, I felt sick inside. This man he started touching me: I was fighting, but he was strong and he put me to a position he wanted me then he pushed himself inside of me.

That day he brought me another man. It was the same thing: more touching and sex. I felt myself dirty and the men hurt me. After that day it was worse. The man brought me more and more men — I do not remember how many. It was this way for many weeks.

One day, I was feeling such pain, such terrible pain. I was

crying, couldn't eat, but still I had to have sex with whoever the man brought me. Then at night he came with another customer. And I said: 'I can't do it with him. I am having my period – I cannot have sex now.' I said that I needed a painkiller tablet.

The men talked in their own language, and the customer left. The boss man went to another room and was talking on the telephone; I was left in the living room. Normally when the boss man come into the place he would lock the door and keep the key with him. But when the customer went out, the key was left in the door.

My heart started beating. I thought: Can I make it? Can I escape?

So I stood up and went to the toilet room. I flushed the toilet because I hoped this would make cover for any noise I would make in getting out of the building. I opened the door very carefully and then went so quietly down the stairs.

As soon as I was outside, I just ran on to the road. I saw some men and I asked them for the police station. They said: 'Just go straight to the traffic lights and turn right.' I ran as fast as I could in that direction. I was so scared that the boss man was behind me and so I rushed inside the police station. The policemen they asked me questions and I was crying. It took a long time for me to tell my story and for them to believe me but after many hours they brought me to this shelter. I am here three days and it is good, but I do not know whether I am safe here. I do not know what has happened to the boss man who tricked me to come here and I am afraid that he will come back to get me and that I will be made to do dirty things with men again.

When Mardea finished her story, she stood upright, quickly and without making eye contact. Unlike Susanna, there was no emotion on her face. As I write this, I know what you are thinking: 'Surely, if this girl is telling the truth, she would be crying and weeping? There would be emotion by the bucket load, not this matter-of-fact account of cynical and brutal rape?'

No, you're wrong. It doesn't work like that: not always. If you had met me here 15 years ago, what would you have seen? Would the Sarah Forsyth you spoke to be a Susanna or a Mardea? Honestly, I can't tell you that I would have been either. I think, I really think, that I could have been like Susanna one day, and Mardea the next. Because what they are dealing with – what I went through – is so terrible that the mind finds ways to shut down: it flicks a switch somewhere inside so that the face goes blank and emotions are anaesthetised.

If you had seen me like this, would you have cared about me? Or would you only care if I cried and writhed, and curled up in a ball? Please listen, don't doubt what I am about to tell you. Mardea is just as damaged – possibly more so – than Susanna. Just as damaged as I have been. And they – and I – need your understanding and your love.

I wonder, too, as you read this, whether any of these stories surprise or shock you. Do they seem outlandish, impossible, and too bad to be true? Do you think, perhaps, that while these stories are terrible, they are isolated instances of wickedness, preying on human vulnerability? Is that what you thought – what you think – of me?

I hope not. Oh, I hope not. Because the truth is that we

– Susanna, Mardea, me – in fact, all the broken and abused women you have met in this book, are not the exceptions: we are the rule. Could this be true? Can human beings really be so evil – and how do I know, anyway? Maybe I'm doing what Karina Schaapman was accused of doing: projecting my own vicious experience on to a picture, which is far more benign? No, I'm not – and here's how I know this.

Do you remember the dossier that Karina Schaapman and her colleague put together in 2008? That investigation for Amsterdam City Council into the reality of its prostitution industry (and, let's be in no doubt, a business that brings to the city an estimated €83 million per year is unquestionably an industry)? What you don't know is that there was a second part to the research – an appendix that included the details of 80 separate pimps controlling prostitutes. Each of these men – and they were all men – was clearly and carefully identified from the testimony of former and current sex slaves; each was alleged to have used violence – sometimes extreme violence – to keep their victims working. This list was handed to Amsterdam police. What happened to it? We shall see; oh, yes, we shall see… but not quite yet.

Because there are other reports you need to know about. Properly researched, scientifically studied investigations into the brave, clean new world of legal prostitution in the Netherlands. Will you look at them with me? One states that 40 per cent of prostitutes here reported experiencing sexual violence; 60 per cent reported physical assault, and 70 per cent reported a verbal threat of a physical assault.

Another reported that anywhere between 50 per cent and 90 per cent of women working in the legal prostitution industry had either been trafficked to the Netherlands or otherwise forced to sell their bodies. Each of those women is a Susanna or a Mardea, or a Sarah Forsyth. Each of them is a human being, with feelings and needs and rights – yes, rights. Each of them is raped on a daily basis by men with the cash to pay sex-slavers for the right to invade another's body.

And you know the really scary thing about these reports? Did you see that little phrase 'the legal prostitution industry'? Every city in the Netherlands that has a visible, legal prostitution sector knows that there is, hidden in the shadows, an *illegal* one. That there are women – God knows how many, for no one is able to count them – who nobody sees. Nobody, that is, except the men who fuck them and forget them, and the traffickers who pocket the proceeds. If all of this violence, this coercion, this trafficking can take place in the legal and visible sector, what on earth happens in the illegal one?

I know the answer to that, and so do you, if you read my last book.[2] Women die. They are broken and beaten, they are trafficked and traded – and they die. Am I angry? Oh, God yes, I'm angry! So, do you care? Well, let's see, shall we?

Let's be tourists. Let us take that cheap, bargain air trip to Amsterdam. What do tourists do when they come to a new city? Why, they most usually pick up the local city guides. Shall we do that, you and I?

From brothels to sex shops to museums, the Red Light District leaves nothing to the imagination. It is very likely that you will have heard about this neighbourhood and to be frank, everything you will have heard is probably true, but to really put the rumours to rest, you have got to check it out for yourself. The Rosse Burt, as the locals know it, is unlike any other place. Guaranteed.

Certainly, the Red Light District that everyone knows about is the one where women of all nationalities parade their wares in red-fringed window parlours, many ready to offer more than a schoolboy peepshow in a private cabin. Another familiar image of the Red Light District is of packs of men, young and old; couples holding hands and pointing in shock of it all; giggling groups of women celebrating a hen night, and busloads of Japanese tourists toting cameras (except not in the direction of the female entertainers – strictly banned!). Proof enough that the RLD deserves a visit, if not a little look-in.

Type 'Amsterdam' into Google and this is one of the first (of many) city guides that will offer themselves to you. This is a commercial website – it makes its money from the Red Light District hotels advertising on it.

Amsterdam prides itself, and rightly so, on its wholly liberal and tolerant attitude, embracing the fact that people may be into prostitution, soft drugs and pornography – and this is only human. So instead of criminalizing everything, this very upfront city wears its heart on its sleeve – what you see is generally what you get. Enjoy the honesty of it all, as you won't find it anywhere else.

Now you tell me: is 'honesty' a word you're comfortable with? How 'honest' do you think was what happened to Susanna, to Mardea, to me? Oh well, you say: this is a commercial website. It's there to sell Amsterdam to tourists and it wouldn't make any money if it told the truth about women like us. Maybe, just maybe: if you can hold your nose long enough, I guess you won't care about the smell, just so long as it puts folding money in your wallet.

But does that excuse work for Amsterdam itself? Surely the city's own tourist information website, *I Amsterdam*, paints a truer picture – one with warts as well as beauty? Well, yes it does – sort of.

The heart of Amsterdam is alive: it is unique and dynamic. It is one of the most beautiful, largest and best kept city centres in the world. It boasts streets and alleyways full of character, as well as fascinating canals and historic buildings. There are interesting churches and museums and a huge diversity of cafés, restaurants and small shops.

The district 'de Wallen' ('the Quays' in English) is known as the *Red Light District*. Prostitutes can be seen in a number of streets in this world-famous district.

The area has historically been an important centre

of prostitution: the district was assigned to prostitutes for the plying of their trade as long ago as 1413. This part of the city centre has always been a special place; a mix of chic and shady.

The majority of people have heard about Amsterdam's Red Light District well before their visit. Leaving nothing to the imagination, some stereotypes about this area are true: there are plenty of sex shops, peep shows, brothels, an elaborate condom shop, a sex museum and prostitutes in red-lit windows.

Now, tell me: does that sound like a city that is concerned – or one that is happy to entice tourists to come and fill Amsterdam's coffers with their money, no matter what the true cost?

Of course that's not the whole story. Amsterdam's website – paid for, remember, by the people and the businesses based there – does contain some acknowledgement that not everything is rosy in De Rosse Burt.

Let's be honest: The Amsterdam city centre has a romantic image. But behind the exciting, unconventional, 'anything goes' image of the city centre lurks a different reality – a reality that sometimes consists of sex trafficking – forced prostitution. This is something that the city and the justice department are fighting against.

Prostitution has enjoyed a long tradition of tolerance in Amsterdam. Safety is key here. In addition to preventing forced prostitution, the aim is an open and honest approach. Sex-workers here have their own union, plenty of police protection, an information centre (for visitors as well), frequent monitoring and testing and professional standards.

You have met Susanna and Mardea; you have listened to Patricia Perquin and Karina Schaapman. Jerrol Martens and Harold van Gelder have shared their expertise. How well do you think Amsterdam is living up to its promise of 'an open and honest approach'? I know what I think: the city wants to have its cake and eat it. It wants you to think that it cares about the women selling their bodies in its windows, while at the same time reaping the rewards of attracting millions of tourists to the Red Light District every year. You think I'm being unfair? Tucked away in the middle of *I Amsterdam* is a telling warning.

Not everything goes. There are certain rules in place to ensure the safety of prostitutes and visitors to the Red Light District. It is forbidden to take photos of the women, and this is strictly enforced.

Stop and think about that for a minute. Have you ever been to a tourist destination – at least one in the 'free' world – where you're not allowed to take photos? You can snap away outside Buckingham Palace, the White House, the Taj Mahal – just about anywhere you care to think of. Except the Red Light District in Amsterdam. Now why is that?

According to Harold van Gelder it's to protect the women as well as the men who make money from them: 'It's not only for the pimps but also for the prostitutes that are working there. It is still a legal profession but with double a morality.

'There is still a taboo – there is still a group of women that work as a prostitute because they earn a lot of money or they have other problems, and when you enter with a camera on nationwide television they won't like it and of course they will get furious and say, "Why are you filming me? What about my privacy?"

'I agree that you should be able to do that but I have experienced several times when I walk around with journalists that this problem is occurring but the people who work and live there don't want to be associated with this camera.'

Like I say, Harold van Gelder is a good, honest and decent man but he's talking rubbish. I was trapped behind those windows and if I'd been in any state to think about it, I would have welcomed someone taking my picture and showing it on English television. Why? Because someone, somewhere, would have recognised me and done something to get me out of that Hell.

No, it's not really the women who are being protected: it's the pimps. They run the streets of the Red Light District. What they say goes, and what they say is no cameras or almost none. Almost. In 2008, a Dutch company set itself up to sell 'unique' tourist package trips. I'm not about to give them free publicity by naming the site, but here's what they offer.

Red Light Sex Trips is about tourists coming over to the Red Light District in Amsterdam to have sex with a pre-booked hooker. They are given a tour by our team of tour-operators through the Red Light District past sex shops, coffee shops and peepshows to the pre-booked hooker.

This site offers you the unique opportunity to book a girl that exactly matches your preferences. For example, would you like to have sex with a blonde MILF with big tits and a round ass doggystyle? Fill out this form and our team will set it up. After submitting your form you'll get a link by email to confirm your booking. After this confirmation you're added to our list of pending sex tourists. Our team processes this list looking for the best possible match.

But our interest isn't so much in this commercial meat-market approach, it's in what follows.

Looking for a matching hooker, taking the guided tour and having sex with the hooker doesn't cost the tourist any money, but in return we want to make a film of your sex trip. That's the deal. After the tour the tourists get a souvenir and after editing a DVD of his/her sex trip is sent home.

Filming is not prohibited, it's a public area, but the hookers behind the window and their pimps don't like being filmed. We respect that, so we don't film them close up without their permission. To not cause any trouble we have our bag with a secret hole in it where we hide our camera. Of course the pre-booked hookers know that we will come and film, this has been prearranged.

So, filming or photography in the Red Light District isn't allowed when it's done to expose the truth, but it's absolutely fine if it helps someone make yet more money from a woman's body. Double-standards? That's Amsterdam.

I don't hate the Netherlands or the Dutch people. Honestly, I don't. But despite all the claims of tolerance and respect for human rights, the reality of the sex business here is the polar opposite to the claims of free and happy hookers that led politicians in this country to legalise prostitution. And you know what? They know this. The people who made the laws legalising the selling of women's bodies, legalising the brothels they get trapped in and the pimps who trick or brutalise them into working behind the windows – all of them know that there has been only one major result: an increase in sex trafficking.

How can I be so sure? Because Werner ten Kate says so: 'We thought in 2000 that say the more liberal view to prostitution would stamp out trafficking, but that proved to be wrong. Everyone thought that, but it worked the other way round.'

If anyone knows the truth, it's Werner ten Kate. Because he's the Dutch government's National Public Prosecutor for Trafficking in Human Beings and People Smuggling.

Up until two years ago, Werner believed the Dutch policy of legalisation had worked, that trafficking of sex slaves into the Netherlands had been stopped. But then a file landed on his neat and tidy desk: it was headed 'Saban Baran'.

Do you remember the photographs we started with – the four frames from a CCTV camera at Schiphol airport and the photos of young and brutalised women in a police station? Those pictures were clipped to the inside of the file. And Werner ten Kate knew that the idealised dream of legal prostitution was over.

Saban Baran and his brother Hassan were – are – Turkish citizens. But despite the fact that as Turks they have no right to work in the European Union, they managed to set up and operate a multi-million Euro prostitution business in Germany and the Netherlands. And this was no illicit, backstreet enterprise: the Baran brothers worked within the legal and licensed sex industry in both countries. Nor was it small-scale. The Baran brothers employed their mother and sister as high-ranking organisers, had more than 130 women working for them as prostitutes, constantly monitored and controlled by dozens of street-level 'operatives'.

'This whole group was formed by up to 50 people, but the core of the group was considered to be 10 members. Some 120–150 women were involved. And a lot of money was involved: we figured out that they have earned about €18–19 million in some six years,' revealed Werner ten Kate.

Think about those numbers: €18 or 19 million. Even with the most conservative arithmetic, it means that each of the women controlled by the Saban gang had to have sex with at least 500 men a year. Can you imagine that?

Imagine 500 men using your body in one year and then another 500 men the year after, and another 500 the year after that. Do you honestly believe these women – any woman – would do so voluntarily? Of course not – because it wasn't the case.

Operating in plain sight, the Baran brothers trafficked women into Holland from all over Eastern Europe. They also bought previously trafficked women from other pimps. And they forced them to sell their bodies in legal Red Light Districts – the very places where police monitoring is meant to be the most stringent.

So, how did they force them? Ask Werner ten Kate.

'They behaved in a very brutal way. Girls were beaten up and to hide bruises, they were put in cold water until the swelling went down. I can show you pictures of girls who didn't behave as the gang wanted them to, who were found by the police the next morning on the street with black eyes and really terrible beatings. But these girls were so afraid that straight away, they started working again for the Baran gang.'

Hassan Baran was the brains behind the operation; Saban was the enforcer – 'the brute force' as the file on Werner ten Kate's desk describes him. The file, which includes 50,000 statements and the transcripts of hours of tapped telephone calls, describes incident after incident of violent beatings. Saban Baran repeatedly slammed one girl's head in a door until her nose was broken because she refused – at first – to sell her body. Another was attacked by the gang with metal baseball bats because she hadn't earned them enough money.

Werner ten Kate picks up the photographs from the file and goes on to explain: 'These ones from the airport camera: they show one of the women who was trying to get away. She had gone to Schiphol to try and get a plane to her home. Saban Baran is the big man who comes to her: he is grabbing her and stopping her from running away.

'The same girl is the one in the police station photographs. They show what Baran did to her – the bruising and the beating around her face. It was very, very brutal.'

And it wasn't just beating. Baran's victims were forced to have cheap breast enlargements and lip enhancements to make themselves more attractive to the men who passed their neon-lit windows. And to ensure his 'merchandise' was not stolen from him by other pimps, Baran had the gang's brand tattooed on their backs.

Women who became pregnant were made to undergo abortions. If they refused, Baran threatened to 'kick their babies out of their stomachs'. And just for good measure, the Baran gang threatened to kill not just any woman who tried to escape, but her family back home in Romania, Moldova or the Czech Republic.

Tell me: if this isn't slavery, what is? And now tell me: how could it be that this happened for three years – three years – in legal, licensed brothels without any of the police spotting it?

'It was this that changed the whole attitude towards the problem we were facing,' continues Werner ten Kate. 'We were not considering actually it to be a problem before that time. But it was the violence and the scale of this in places where everything was supposed to be regulated quite well which made us believe that legalised prostitution has actually contributed to sex trafficking, not stopped it. The three cities they were working in – Amsterdam, Utrecht and Alkmaar – have relatively large prostitution areas, so it was all too easy for the gang to bring women in for prostitution there.

'Because of this case we found out that between 60–70 per cent of women are being forced to work in legalised prostitution scenes, so that changed the whole attitude towards this problem. And now we are at the moment that we think the liberal system has been too much, and the clock is turning the other way around now.'

The more I heard about the Baran gang, the more I thought of my time here in Amsterdam's Red Light District. I was sold by my first trafficker to a Yugoslavian gang just like the Barans. They too were quick to use violence to keep 'their women' in line. And there was something else, tucked away in the back of Werner ten Kate's file: the leader of the Yugoslavs who traded in my flesh owned and ran one of Amsterdam's licensed 'coffee shops' – the ones legally selling cannabis and hashish to tourists. That was how he also dealt in cocaine and eventually got me hooked on crack. Saban Baran's indictment – because he was eventually arrested and charged – shows that he and his brother owned at least one of these 'coffee shops' (as well as sex shops and brothels).

We need to look at that indictment for Saban Baran; we need to see the extent of his crimes: sex trafficking, extortion, aggravated assault, rape, drug trafficking, leading a criminal organisation and attempted murder. All based on and around legalised prostitution.

Some people might say that the Baran case proves that the system does eventually catch brutal sex-slavers, 'eventually' being the word. And it's true that a court sentenced the Barans and their gang to up to 15 years each – though under the quaint Dutch legal custom of not identifying convicted criminals, you'd be hard pushed to find out. But that's not the whole story – no, not the whole story at all.

Saban Baran was meant to serve seven-and-a-half years in prison and ordered to pay €100,000 in lieu of another year behind bars, but prisons in Holland allow inmates to have conjugal visits and even to marry. One of Baran's prostitutes came to the prison, took part in a wedding ceremony and had sex with him. You can guess what happened next.

In September 2009, a baby was born. Saban Baran applied for 'compassionate leave' to visit his newborn child. This being the Netherlands, a court in Arnheim agreed – despite the objections of police and prosecutors. Saban Baran, convicted sex trafficker, violent pimp and drug trafficker, was allowed to walk out of the prison gates on the promise that he would return the next day. Instead he fled to Turkey, which conveniently has no extradition agreement with the Netherlands. He was last seen running a 'nightclub' in the southern Turkish tourist resort of Antalya.

The more I thought about Saban Baran, the more I

remembered someone else – someone more than 1,000 miles away. Someone we have already met, you and I.

Alexandr 'Salun' Kovali will rot in a shabby Moldova prison for another 18 years. Moldova – the poorest country in Europe, which struggles to pay its police, let alone keep them free of corruption – managed to lock up a major international sex trafficker, who was shipping women out of the country.

Saban Baran can stroll up and down the beach at Antalya, free as a bird, because the Netherlands – one of the richest countries in Europe, with a police force dedicated to locking up sex-slavers who import women – allowed him to walk free.

Now you tell me: which country takes sex trafficking more seriously?

You don't have to have been a sex-trafficked woman; you don't have to have gone through the same ordeal as me to spot the simple economic truth. Where there is demand, there will be supply. And all that legalising prostitution has achieved is to give sex traffickers better cover. But don't take it from me: take it from Jerrol Martens, the man who runs the Netherland's national trafficking reporting organisation.

Jerrol explained: 'Everyone knows Holland is famous for its Red Light Districts, that's not only in Amsterdam but throughout the country. We have Red Light windows, brothels, private sex houses, saunas, massage, couples' clubs, swingers' clubs, and prostitution is allowed in all of them. That means there is a demand for young girls here, and I think that traffickers make use of our system of legalised prostitution to bring them in from other countries. Because of the EU open borders, they come in by car, by bus, by air, by boat… by any means.

'It is above ground, so it is easy to use our laws to import women, and once the traffickers have the women here, they can misuse the system and trade in these women to other countries. The Netherlands is really the passport to trafficking women into the rest of Europe.'

I couldn't have put it better myself.

But before we leave the Netherlands and its Red Light Districts of licensed, legal sex slavery, there's one more person I want you to meet. His name is John Miller and he's not actually in the Netherlands, but he knows it – oh yes, he knows it all too well. Until 2008, John Miller was the world's top anti-slavery official. He worked for the President of the United States, running America's global anti-trafficking efforts.

We'll come to those later in our journey, but for now what you need to know is that the reason they exist at all is that John Miller argued and fought, lobbied and pleaded until the US government listened. And one of the first places he visited? Amsterdam. 'I went to the Red Light District. I watched the young men with their leather jackets standing outside those windows, counting who goes in and making sure they get all the profits. I know what I saw: it was sex slavery. And I heard what the government in the Netherlands told me, about how legalised prostitution would stop sex trafficking.

'You know, the Dutch believe that they're being very sophisticated and regulating this way but the interesting thing is that this is the exact same approach they took back in the 17th century when the slave trade was at its height. The Dutch used to boast about how they had the healthiest slave ships: they had the best ventilation, they had the best rations, they had the best mattresses for their slaves, and they provided doctors. Ah, but slavery went on and on: all their talk about regulation was an excuse to avoid abolition.

'With regards to sex slavery, I think all that's happened is that the Dutch government has become a "super pimp".'

---

[1] In late 2011, Toos left the Scarlet Cord to open the Amsterdam office of Not For Sale (www.notforsalecampaign.org), one of the leading international anti-slavery organisations. She still visits and campaigns for the women in the windows. *See Afterword*.

[2] In *Slave Girl* (John Blake Publishing Limited, 2009), Sarah describes witnessing the murder of a Thai girl, trafficked to Amsterdam's then illicit Red Light District.

CHAPTER EIGHT

SEEING RED

I am angry. I am home – now far from the sorrow of Moldova and the industrialised rape of women in Europe's legal sex industry. I am in my flat in dull, quiet Gateshead. And I'm angry – a deep, inner and rumbling fury.

Perhaps you're thinking that it's what we have seen together, the women we have met and the men who enslaved them, which has provoked this anger. And it has – of course it has. I hope that you too have been shocked. But it's not Chişinău or De Rosse Burt in Amsterdam that has made me see red: it's an article in a British newspaper.

The *Guardian* isn't, I freely admit, my usual choice of reading – I don't tend to buy broadsheet papers. But I do know that it's one of the best and most responsible newspapers in the country. Which made what follows all the worse.

PROSTITUTION AND TRAFFICKING – THE ANATOMY OF A MORAL PANIC
By Nick Davies
October 2009

There is something familiar about the tide of misinformation which has swept through the subject of sex trafficking in the UK: it flows through exactly the same channels as the now notorious torrent about Saddam Hussein's weapons. In the story of UK sex trafficking, the conclusions of academics who study the sex trade have been subjected to the same treatment as the restrained reports of intelligence analysts who studied Iraqi weapons – stripped of caution, stretched to their most alarming possible meaning and tossed into the public domain.

There, they have been picked up by the media who have stretched them even further in stories which have then been treated as reliable sources by politicians, who in turn provided quotes for more misleading stories.

In both cases, the cycle has been driven by political opportunists and interest groups in pursuit of an agenda. In the case of sex trafficking, the role of the neo-conservatives and Iraqi exiles has been played by an unlikely union of evangelical Christians with feminist campaigners, who pursued the trafficking tale to secure their greater goal, not of regime change, but of legal change to abolish all prostitution. The sex trafficking story is a model of misinformation.

Saddam Hussein? Misinformation? Political opportunists? Do these words bear any relation to – let alone accurately describe – the stories of the women we already met? The women in Carl Pritchett's Birmingham brothels? The poor, bewildered Nigerian girls trapped in sex slavery in 'massage parlours' and 'saunas' across Ireland, too terrified to do anything about their plight because they had been forced to undergo voodoo rituals – rituals which you and I might find absurd but which they believed to be very real.

Moral panic? Real panic – genuine, paralysing fear maybe. But 'moral panic', a fantasy dreamed up by Christians and feminists? How on earth can anyone – especially a responsible, serious newspaper – print this rubbish?

But it got worse.

Research published recently by Dr Nick Mai of London Metropolitan University concludes that, contrary to public perception, the majority of migrant sex workers have chosen prostitution as a source of 'dignified living conditions and to increase their opportunities for a better future while dramatically improving the living conditions of their families in the country of origin'.

After detailed interviews with 100 migrant sex workers in the UK, Mai found: 'For the majority, working in the sex industry was a way to avoid the exploitative working conditions they had met in their previous non-sexual jobs.'

Read that again to yourself. Slowly. Try and match the phrases 'dignified living conditions' and 'a better future' to the experiences of the women we've met who were imported to Britain as sex slaves. Can you do it? I can't – I bloody well can't.

I don't doubt for a moment that there are some women who come to this country (or to the Netherlands and or Spain, or Germany for that matter) deliberately determined to sell their bodies. And I'm equally sure that for those women, the money they make – assuming it isn't snatched from them by a pimp – is more than they would make in a poor country like Moldova. But I've been a whore: hundreds and hundreds of men fucked me for money and I'll tell you, the *Guardian* and that researcher from the University the simple truth. Willing or unwilling, there's no dignity in having to open your mouth or your legs for anyone with a bit of spare cash. There's no future in having your body abused and re-abused, day after day after day. The myth of the Happy Hooker – for that's what is being conjured up here – is just that: a myth.

And yes, I am angry.

I thought, I honestly thought, that we had got past that in this country but apparently not. So it seems we need to look again at what happens in our towns and cities, what happens in plain sight on our streets: we need to listen again.

Let's start in Ireland. Just as in Britain no one knows how many prostitutes work there but we do know some of them don't do so willingly; some have been trafficked into the country by violent organised crime gangs. How do we know? Because we know about Florin Nicolae Ghinea, that's how.

Nicolae is a burly, heavily-tattooed Romanian thug. He has a criminal record that includes violent attacks and money laundering, and he has built up relationships with other criminal networks in his home country and overseas. Police in Romania describe him as 'an exceptionally violent group leader'.

He was first arrested in Nice in 2003. Dogged detective work by French police showed that for the previous three years, he orchestrated the smuggling of prostitutes from Eastern Europe into Spain and France. A court in Nice sentenced him to seven years for aggravated pimping and human trafficking: after a brief spell in a French prison he was allowed to serve the remainder of his jail term back home in Romania.

Romanian jails must be a little less strict than those in other parts of Europe because Nicolae managed to carry on his business, organising the shipment of yet more young women from Eastern Europe. This time, though, they were sent to work in brothels in Dublin and Galway. And all the time Nicolae was micro-managing the operation from his prison cell with constant updates on the women involved, the 'cargo' being shipped and the money made.

When he got out of jail, after serving just five years of his sentence, the business grew and grew. Indeed, it became so big that it came to the notice of the organised crime division of Romania's Ploiesti Brigade. Between 2008 and January 2009, the division documented the gang's offences across Europe – cybercrime, human trafficking for sexual exploitation, money laundering, blackmail, robbery, fraud and kidnapping.

In April 2009, in a joint operation with Irish police, they raided 11 houses and found 10 young women, who were described as having 'model good looks'. The women in Romania had just arrived back from Ireland, where they had been forced to sell their bodies in a string of linked brothels.

Does that sound like a 'moral panic'? Or does it sound very familiar: violent organised criminals enslaving vulnerable young women in commercial brothels?

And what about north of the border? Let's drive up the N1 motorway from Dublin to Belfast. Let's meet Rong Chen.

In July 2012, Chen – who lived in the pleasant town of Kidderminster, on the edge of one of England's most beautiful forests – was sentenced to seven years imprisonment for trafficking women from China to Northern Ireland and forcing them to become prostitutes by threatening to murder them if they refused.

Chen hooked her victims with adverts in Chinese newspapers promising relatively well-paid jobs as childminders in Northern Ireland. Instead they were taken to squalid flats before being shuttled between at least five brothels in Belfast, Newry in Co Down and Londonderry. Chen told the women her husband was a Chinese Triad gang leader, threatened them with extreme violence and boasted that she had high-level police contacts to protect her. At least part of that was true. Alongside Chen in the dock were her husband, Jason Hinton, and Simon

Dempsey, a former policeman from Northern Ireland. Hinton was given a community service; Dempsey was jailed for nine months.

The judge, Mr Justice Stephens, told Chen that she had regarded her victims' well-being as 'inconsequential' – 'You sexually exploited and degraded women as a commodity for financial gain, irrespective of the impact on them and their lives. There was coercion involved in that you, Rong Chen, coerced four of the women who worked in these brothels.'

Can you imagine the terror of those young Chinese women, conned into believing they were going to work with children, then forced with threats of violence to allow men to have sex with them for money? I can: it happened to me, to the letter.

One of the side-effects of finally getting clear of my past – coming off methadone, kicking the booze and ridding myself of Hepatitis C – was that for the first time I could face reading all the responses to my story. It was an extraordinary feeling: the vast majority of you who took the time to write about what you'd read – and there were hundreds of readers – were wonderfully supportive. Despite all the cold, hard evidence of my own bad behaviour, letter after letter was filled with kindness, sympathy and love. I can't ever thank you enough, or put into words how much this has meant to me. To know that so many people care enough to respond so positively is one of the planks on which I have built my recovery.

Of course there were others who doubted my story and who – much like that *Guardian* article – couldn't or wouldn't believe that an innocent young girl could be tricked and trafficked from England to the cesspit of Amsterdam's Red Light District. However much these responses – some expressed in pretty blunt terms – hurt me, I don't blame the writers. The facts are there: John Reece, the man who first conned and then sold me into sex slavery, was convicted and that's a matter of public record. But I know it is difficult to understand, let alone accept, that this callous depravity actually happens. So, for those of you who did doubt – and to those of you who have helped me on my journey – we need to meet someone else now.

Anthony Harrison came to England in April 2003. Arriving at Heathrow, he claimed to be from Liberia, the West African country established in the 19th century as a colony for freed American slaves. In reality, he was from Nigeria and involved with an established trafficking gang, which shipped human cargo from Africa to Europe. Although his asylum application was refused, he managed to stay in Britain and find work – under one of several false names he adopted – as a caretaker in the London Borough of Newham.

But Harrison's real business was sex trafficking. He took over the British end of the existing operation and arranged for the first of his victims to be sent to London. What you're about to read took two long years for the police to coax out of those victims. Two years in which they were so terrified of what would happen to them that they barely spoke a word.

The two girls were aged 14 and 16. I can't tell you their

names because – quite rightly – they are being protected. We can call them only 'Girl A' and 'Girl B'. Young and vulnerable children, originally they lived in small villages in Edo, an inland province of Nigeria. Girl A was brought up by her uncle, who physically and sexually abused her. Girl B was abandoned by a river as a baby and taken in by the man who found her but she was treated as a 'domestic drudge' and frequently beaten.

From these sad beginnings the girls were then sold into prostitution with the help of a local Juju priest. However outlandish this might seem to us, Juju is a significant part of West African culture and particularly prevalent in the Edo State of Nigeria: people in the villages believe in it, just as they believe in other religions like Christianity. If someone falls ill and dies, or even if there's some general misfortune affecting a family member, people believe someone else has used the power of Juju to put a curse on them.

Anthony Harrison's trafficking gang preyed on this primal fear.

Girl A endured a ritual in which she was stripped and cut with a razor blade so her blood could be collected. Her body hair was shaved off and she was forced to lie naked in a closed coffin for hours. She then had to eat a raw chicken heart.

Girl B was taken to a river, where she was told to eat white clay, had a rock passed from a priest's mouth to hers, was given black soap to wash with and a raw chicken's egg to eat. The rituals had a cynical purpose: to instil the maximum amount of terror, and imprint on these two very vulnerable young women that they should not step out of line or give any information about what happened to them.

Girl A was trafficked to the UK in May 2009, when under her handler's instructions she went to Anthony Harrison's flat. He promptly imprisoned her for six days before giving her false ID, a mobile phone and a plane ticket to Spain; he also gave her a script to follow if she was questioned by anyone. Arriving at Madrid airport, she was stopped by suspicious immigration officials. After they discovered that her documents were bogus, they sent her back to the UK.

When British police began to question Girl A, she kept to the script Harrison had given her, saying she had fled her village in Nigeria and sought sanctuary in a church after being accused of being a lesbian. She claimed she had been brought to the UK by a man called 'Reverend Francis' – but more than that she would not, or could not, say.

It would take long and painfully patient interviews with specially trained police officers before she began – haltingly and a small bit at a time – to talk about the rituals she had endured, and the sheer terror they had instilled in her. The police would later release sections of a taped interview with this poor, frightened 16-year-old girl. In one of them a female officer is heard asking: 'Do you still think that you're going to die from talking to the police?' And the girl replies:

That's what they told me, but I don't know. At that time, I believed it – even till now – because people are scared of it and they said it kill people. I always believed that if I talked to the police I will die — it was in my head. It's beginning to change because the first time I talk to the police I was waiting: I thought I was gonna die, but I was still waiting. Until now I haven't died.

Girl B was the 14-year-old. She was initially found in August 2009, when a credit card being monitored by police after Girl A was stopped was used to buy an easyJet plane ticket to Athens. At Luton airport, police stopped Girl B, who was carrying identification documents belonging to 'Samantha Jones' the day after she had checked in.

She told police that she had been taken to Lagos to attend school, but had been sold as a prostitute. Girl B was also imprisoned by Harrison before he attempted to sell her on.

With both girls under police supervision in the UK, they should have been safe but with no family to look after them, they were placed in local authority care. Almost immediately, they absconded in order to contact their trafficker: Anthony Harrison.

It took many more months of police investigation and careful interviewing before Harrison was arrested and charged with two counts of conspiracy to traffic people into the UK for sexual exploitation, two of conspiracy to traffic out of the UK for sexual exploitation, two counts of false imprisonment and four of conspiracy to facilitate breaches of immigration law. Not until July 2011 was the case finally closed: a jury at Woolwich Crown Court convicted him and Harrison was sentenced to 20 years behind bars.

It's worth listening to what DC Andy Desmond of the Metropolitan Police's Human Exploitation and Organised Crime Command said that day in July: worth it because what he had to say needed to be said – not just for Girl A and Girl B, but for hundreds, thousands, of other young women tricked, trafficked and then raped over and over in brothels the length and breadth of this country. And it needs saying for me, too: I have known the fear these young girls endured, though mine was caused by a man with a gun and not a Juju priest with paint and feathers.

'I would like to pay tribute to the two victims who showed tremendous courage by talking to the police and agreeing to testify against their captor. These young women suffered the most terrifying and degrading ordeal – leaving them emotionally, psychologically and physically traumatised. Most cruelly of all, they were brainwashed into believing that if they disobeyed their captors by seeking help, they would die. They were also told that if they went to the police for help, they would be handed straight back to their captors.

'I hope that this conviction sends out a strong message to other victims who have suffered similar experiences that you can speak out without fearing for your lives. The Metropolitan Police Service is fully aware of this crime. We will listen to you, we will not dismiss you and we will do all that we can to bring the perpetrators to justice.'

I want to believe this, I really do: I want to believe that this country is committed to watching out for women who have been trafficked into sex slavery. I want to believe that we will listen to them, hear their stories, accept the truth of what they say – but can I? Can you?

Do you remember 'Cuddles' – that grotesquely inappropriately named 'massage parlour' in Birmingham, run by millionaire, Ferrari-driving Carl Pritchett? Well, West Midlands police raided the brothel. So it should be a success story that justifies our hopes. Except it doesn't – just about everything was wrong with the operation.

The police found 19 women in the brothel; 13 of them had EU passports, which – in theory – allowed them to live and work in Britain. They were held in cells for two nights before being released. Because they were 'legal' workers, no one asked whether they had been forced to sell their bodies.

The remaining six women were from Albania, Moldova, Romania and Thailand – all well-known countries of origin for sex trafficking, but outside the EU. This made them illegal immigrants and without any questions being asked, they were hauled off to Yarl's Wood Immigration Removal Centre, ready for deportation. Only last-minute efforts by volunteer lawyers managed to prevent the government from shipping them back to uncertain futures in their home countries. Eventually a representative of the Poppy Project was allowed to meet four of the women. The result – finally, and 12 days after the raid – was that two of these women were identified as sex-trafficking victims. What do you think would have happened if those volunteer lawyers and the workers from the Poppy Project hadn't stepped in? We know the answer, don't we? We've already been to some of these countries and we've met a sex slave who was sent back, just like that. What happened to her? She was sex-trafficked again.

The awful truth is that while cases like Anthony Harrison show that we can get it right, that we can help trafficked women, there are as many cases where we don't

Why? How could we be so blind? Do you really want to know? Because I can tell you. But before I do, I want to ask you a question. Why are you reading this book? Is it because you want a good story? A story of sex and violence, sometimes death, or is it because you care – really care – about why a young girl like me can end up trapped in a Hell of forced prostitution and chained with the invisible bonds of drug addiction? I hope it's that second reason: because if you really want to understand why we have to talk about policies and protocols and all the other boring-sounding stuff that governments churn out, but which they are really all about people.

Will you listen for a while?

We've got lots of policies in this country and we've got lots of different police teams and agencies. And we've got a whole industry built on the backs of women forced to sell sex and, in theory, dedicated to protecting them. And the people who work in these police forces and voluntary groups and charities are incredibly hardworking and doing the best they can, but there's a problem.

Politicians love to spout on about how much this country cares; how we have a great commitment to stamping out sex slavery. But that's not what they mean. If we had one of those translation devices, whenever they talk about stopping sex trafficking we'd hear something completely different. Because what that actually means is that they want to stop immigration. That's why all the laws we use against sex-slavers in Britain talk about 'trafficking'.

And trafficking is about illegal immigration: nothing more, nothing less. Sex slavery is about women being forced – often with violence – to allow men to rape them. Trafficking is just the means to get them here in the first place. And because we concentrate on trafficking, we stop thinking about the slavery. It's that story – *The Elephant and The Blind Men* – all over again.

And how do I know? How does little Sarah Forsyth from Gateshead – ex-crack whore and jailbird – know so much? Because the facts are there in front of us, just like the elephant, if only we'd take off our blindfolds and look, properly look.

Fact number one: in 2009 the government – that's the British government, voted in by you and me – decided to stop funding the Poppy Project. It believed it could get a 'better deal' by handing the responsibility for dealing with trafficked women over to the Salvation Army. Now don't get me wrong, I'm not saying a word against the Sally Ann: they do great work and they're very dedicated people but they're not specialists in sex trafficking. So why did they get the funding? I think I know. The Poppy Project doesn't pull any punches: as well as giving shelter and wonderful support to sex slaves rescued from British brothels, they also say straight out that the existence of these high-street brothels is what drives the demand for importing poor duped girls from Eastern Europe.

Fact two: this government – yours and mine – still doesn't treat sex-trafficking victims properly. If they're found in a brothel here without an EU passport, guess how they're treated? Yes, the instinctive response is to view them as illegal immigrants; as women who have chosen to come here and have their bodies invaded in 'dignified living conditions and to increase their opportunities for a better future while dramatically improving the living conditions of their families in the country of origin' – to quote that university clever-clogs we met earlier.

There's someone else I want you to meet. We'll call her Katya, for reasons you'll understand very quickly. In April 2011, Katya was about to take on the British government in one of the highest courts in the country; that she had to do this is a terrible indictment of the way we treat trafficked women.

Harrow is one of London's wealthiest boroughs: it has a flagship arts centre, a university campus and is home to the second most famous English public school. It was in this fancy part of town that police found Katya, imprisoned in a brothel. She was 18 years old, from Moldova – and terrified.

Katya's story – contained in court documents – should make us all feel ashamed. Ashamed that a young and vulnerable girl could be brought to Britain and forced into prostitution; ashamed that when our government found her it treated her appallingly and put her life in danger.

Katya was 14 when the ordeal began. She was living with her mother in Moldova when two older men invited her and a friend to a birthday picnic in a nearby forest.

Both girls were knocked unconscious and driven across the border to Romania. There they were blindfolded and taken across a river in an inflatable dinghy to somewhere in Hungary. Here, the teenagers were given dark clothing and made to walk, in the dead of night, through the forest across the border and into Slovenia. But this was only another stop along the way: their final destination was to be Italy.

They were sold on to two separate men and told they were to be prostitutes. There was no arguing: these were violent and vicious traffickers. Katya was first made to sell her body in a flat in Rimini – one of Italy's most popular seaside tourist resorts. From there she was taken to Milan and forced to work as a street prostitute. After several months – months in which her teenage body was raped and abused by hundreds of men – she managed to escape. She made her way to the Moldovan Embassy: staff there gave her shelter, she was interviewed by Italian police and then she discovered that she was pregnant.

Katya did what any teenager might do: she told embassy officials that she wanted to go home, to give birth to her child in the safety of the family home. But her traffickers found her: they beat and raped her brother and killed the family dog as punishment for her decision to tell Italian police what had happened to her. They also told her the friend with whom she had been kidnapped had been murdered: the pimps who had prostituted her had drugged the teenager and thrown her off a seven-storey building.

The message was crystal clear: keep your mouth shut and your head down or we'll take revenge on your family.

After she gave birth, Katya sent her daughter to live in relative safety with an aunt. And then the traffickers came back for her. She was sent to Turkey to work in a nightclub. Later, she was smuggled in a lorry to London and put to work in the brothel in Harrow. During her time working as a prostitute, she was given no money and was not allowed to go anywhere unaccompanied in case she tried to escape.

The men who abused her body in the brothel rarely, if ever, asked about the conditions in which she was working; much less did they want to know if she had been forced to let them penetrate her.

The clients, they're drunk, and just come and say, 'Give me this, that.' No one asks, 'How are you?' Some of them asked, 'Why do you do this job?' but I wouldn't answer. I was afraid that if I asked them for help, they might turn out to be friends with my trafficker.

It was the same story with the other women – mainly Eastern European, none of them British. None of them ever talked about how they came to be imprisoned, in plain sight, in the pleasant streets of Harrow.

I didn't know if the other girls were friends of the trafficker. It was dangerous to speak to the clients or the other girls. There were speakers in the flat where we lived. We didn't talk about anything. Sometimes we were locked up for weeks and weeks, not going out.

Along with the other women in the brothel, Katya was arrested when the police finally raided the premises in 2007. The detectives suspected she might have been trafficked but Katya would not talk about it because the Kosovan Albanian man who had bought her made it very clear that her family would be in danger if she said anything to anyone.

She was transferred to a detention centre for illegal immigrants. Because officials there did not realise Katya had been intimidated by her trafficker, they allowed him to visit her on nine separate occasions: he took advantage of this to threaten her again.

She was also visited by British immigration officials. Very quickly they realised that she had been indeed been trafficked and forced into prostitution yet despite this, they decided that she would face no real danger if she was sent back home. They put her on a plane to Chişinău. Within days her traffickers tracked her down to the Moldovan village where she had grown up.

They took me to a forest and I was beaten and raped. Then they made a noose out of rope and told me to dig my own grave as I was going to be killed. They tied the noose around my neck and let me hang before cutting the branch off the tree.

I really believed I was going to die. They then drove me to a house where many men were staying. They were all very drunk and took turns to rape me. When I tried to resist, one man physically restrained me and pulled my front tooth out using pliers.

Katya's attackers stopped short of murdering her – but not out of pity or any sense of humanity. The man who had originally trafficked her told the men to lay off because he wanted to traffick her again. As she put it:

I think maybe they did not kill me because I was more valuable alive.

And she was – oh, she was. First, she was trafficked to Israel and forced to work in a brothel in Tel Aviv. After a few weeks she escaped but was re-captured and trafficked again, this time to London. She was forced to work in a flat in the centre of the city, where her pimps sold her for £150 an hour; she received none of this money. In 2007 she was detained for a second time by immigration officials, who considered returning her to Moldova before finally granting her refugee status.

Katya is now 27. She is thin and pale, but dentists have replaced her tooth and she keeps the other evidence of what was done to her body well hidden.

I think I was lucky. I didn't have too many scars or injuries as the traffickers wanted to keep me looking pretty.

But there are scars which aren't visible on a prostitute's body; wounds which don't heal over with protective scabs of skin. Just as I was, Katya was diagnosed with post-traumatic stress. And just as my mind was ravaged as badly as my body, Katya's brain can't cope with the ordeal she was put through. With the help of the Poppy Project she has been offered specialist counselling but finds the therapy sessions too painful to bear.

You'd think – at least I hope you'd think – that the British government would have been ashamed of the way it behaved. Ashamed that it had sent a brutalised and terrified teenager back into the clutches of her traffickers; ashamed that it allowed – no, *enabled* – them to gang-rape her and re-sell her broken body time and again. You'd think, wouldn't you? But you'd be wrong.

With the help of lawyers, Katya filed a claim for damages against the British government. If it had felt any scrap of shame – or even human decency – an apology would have been issued and Katya would have been given the money she needs to be able to live and in time, heal. Instead it rejected her claim and made her pursue it in the courts.

Can you imagine how that must feel? This girl – because she is just a girl, whose childhood was stolen from her – was forced by the very people who had slung her back to her traffickers to face the daunting prospect of taking on the power and the money of the British government in court.

Over the course of two years Katya was interviewed by medical and trafficking experts in preparation for the trial. All of them found her story completely credible.

Her legal team researched the law and argued that British immigration officials should have investigated evidence that she was a victim of trafficking and that their decision to return her to Moldova, where she ran the risk of retribution and re-trafficking, was a violation of her rights under article 3 (the right to freedom from torture and inhumane and degrading treatment) and article 4 (the right to freedom from slavery and servitude) of the European Convention on Human Rights.

Document after document was filed at the court. In one, the former head of the Metropolitan Police's Vice Unit, Paul Holmes, said that when Katya was first picked up in 2003 there was already plenty of evidence that should have led immigration officials to identify her as a trafficking victim. In a written statement he said there was 'friction' at that time between the immigration service's policy of kicking 'illegal entrants' out of the country, and his department's desire to interview potential victims and get them to testify against traffickers.

'Our doubt about the effectiveness of prompt removal was exacerbated by the fact that our intelligence-gathering and operational activities had highlighted the fact that in some cases, victims that had been removed were subjected to re-trafficking and were being discovered for a second time in London brothels or elsewhere within weeks of their original removal.'

The day before Katya's case was due to open at the high court in London, lawyers for the British government finally gave in: they agreed to pay substantial damages.

Outside the court, Katya's solicitor, Harriet Wistrich, told journalists she hoped the case would highlight the dangers of the way this country deals with trafficked women – and educate people about the reality of the trafficking of women from Eastern Europe: 'People don't believe it's happening on this scale. People don't want to believe it.'

No, they don't. They would prefer to believe that girls like Katya choose to sell their bodies to brutal and selfish men because that way they can 'enjoy' those wonderful 'dignified living conditions'. Now you tell me: does her story bear even the remotest resemblance to that smug academic research we heard at the start of this chapter? And what did the British government say about all this? How did it justify being part of the re-trafficking of a sex slave?

The Home Office issued a statement, claiming that since 2003 there have been 'improvements' in the way immigration officials deal with trafficked women. It said: 'The UK has become a world leader in fighting trafficking and has a strong international reputation in this field.'

Really? In the next chapter we shall see what being 'a world leader' really means. Whatever the theory, in practice the Poppy Project knows that women rescued from British brothels are still being sent back to the countries they came from and re-trafficked. And not just a few women, the occasional case here and there. No, 21 per cent of the women who came to the charity seeking help had already been sent home and re-trafficked at least once.

Maybe it's the refusal to accept the government's comforting claims that underpinned the decision – announced in the same month as Katya was finally given compensation – to strip the Poppy Project of its funding. That's certainly how it looks to Katya:

> If the government cared, it would not be closing the Poppy
> Project. They don't care.

No, they don't. Do you?

Back in Moldova, Katya's traffickers have not been
arrested and she is worried they could now target her
younger sister. For the moment she plans to stay in the UK
and has signed up for computer courses and English
language classes. She is also doing voluntary work. Recently
she succeeded in bringing her daughter to live with her, but
is still terrified that she could run into those who forced her
into prostitution in London. One thing of which she is
certain is that the British police need to do much more to
protect women like her and to prevent others from being
trafficked into prostitution.

> Just look around you — see how many girls there are like me.
> They are coming all the time. I see them every day — in tube
> stations, all made up, early in the morning. Maybe for you it
> is difficult to see them, but I see them. I think the police
> should work harder to stop this. Why don't you shut down
> saunas and brothels? Then there would be no prostitutes,
> no pimps.

It's a good question, isn't it?

But the most amazing thing about this brave young
woman is her willingness to forgive the British government
for the part it played in her ordeal:

> I'm not angry with the government. How can you be angry

with the government? I'm angry with my life, the things that have happened.

I take my hat off to Katya. Because I myself cannot be so forgiving. Am I angry? You bet I am.

CHAPTER NINE

OF ANGELS
AND PINS

How many angels can dance – simultaneously – on the head of a pin?

This ridiculous-sounding question exercised some of the greatest thinkers, philosophers and academics for several hundred years. Lengthy tracts were published considering whether angels had bodies and therefore could dance or whether they were purely spiritual beings that could fit snugly on anything, in unlimited number. But the correct answer, of course, is a series of questions: what do we mean by 'angel'? How vigorously are they dancing? And just how big is the pin?

No, I haven't lost my mind: there's a point to all this. Today in our modern, largely secular world, the Angels and Pins debate has come to be used as a sort of shorthand for pointless speculation – a medieval equivalent of the 'How many people does it take to change a lightbulb?' joke.

So here's a question: How many countries does it take to stop sex trafficking and sex slavery? And the answer? It's that same old set of questions: What do we mean by 'sex'? How do we define 'trafficking' and what exactly is 'slavery' in this context? You see where I'm going with this?

It should be so simple. Everyone agrees that slavery is wrong: after all, no one votes to make sex trafficking legal. But no one can agree what the individual words mean, much less who should tackle them, or how. But we have to start somewhere, so we're going to start at the centre of the worldwide struggle to make slavery history.

Washington DC is an impressive city. It was specifically built to be impressive. After America declared independenc in 1776, the new government set about creating a capital that would give the impression of power and inspire awe in foreign statesmen and dignitaries.

Number 1600 Pennsylvania Avenue sits squarely in the middle of downtown DC. We know it better by its universal name: The White House. And behind the pillars and porticos we see on television news, it's the man in the Oval Office who is the most important figure in the global fight to protect women like Katya and Susanna, Mardea and me from the men who enslaved us.

As I write, Barack Obama has just won his second term in office as US President. The news is awash with images of a black man in the ultimate seat of power – a man who 150 years ago would have been sold as a slave on the street corner opposite the White House. But the reason why the United States has come to lead the fight against slavery in all its modern forms isn't an African-American in the Oval Office today: it's a tall, gangling man who walked in there 10 years ago and dared to bang on the Presidential desk.

The first thing you notice about John Miller is that his arms and legs are constantly in motion, splaying out wildly as he rams a point home. Then you realise how he came to be appointed as the US 'anti-slavery Czar': determination. Never one to shrink from a fight, he quickly sized up the fundamental problem: 'Slavery exists in every country in the world including the United States. Of course it's hard to measure how many slaves there are because you don't take a census and slaves don't raise their hands and answer 'I'm a slave', but there are many, many millions.

'And yet nobody is in favour of slavery. We know that, right? But some people are willing to act and some aren't. Some governments are willing to be aggressive and some governments look the other way and make excuses – I wasn't going to have that.'

Miller knew enough to realise he couldn't stop the modern slave trade altogether but he was determined to at least put a spoke in its wheels. But the harder he worked, the more frustrated he became: 'Everyone everywhere was having big international conferences about the problem. Well, I discovered that these multi-lateral conferences were great for getting academic papers published, and first-class at having everybody say how terrible modern slavery is, but they didn't accomplish anything. I went to one conference after my first three months in the job and that was the last one I went to because I realised it didn't do a darn bit of good.'

So, instead of jetting round the world to sit and talk about people like Katya and Susanna, Mardea and me, he did something completely different. He talked to us.

'The one who sticks in my mind is a girl I met in Amsterdam: name of Anika, originally from the Czech Republic. At the age of 18 she was convinced by a friend – who was really no friend at all – to travel to the Netherlands for a job. Well, the people who promised the job turned out to be traffickers.

'They took several Czech girls and they took them to a brothel. Anika said: "I don't wanna do this, I came to work in a restaurant." But they said: "You'll work here: if you wanna leave, you owe us €20,000." So Anika had to stay there and work in that brothel for years.

'And I wanted to know how this could happen. I mean, Holland is a good country, a rich country. It's disgusting, but I'll tell you what was even more upsetting: the reaction of different people. When I asked the non-governmental organisations how many people in the Red Light District do you think are in slavery, they said: "Oh, about 80 per cent." When I asked the head of the Dutch Sex Trafficking office, she said: "Oh, maybe 15 per cent." When I asked the head of the Dutch police department that was involved in this issue, he said 40 or 50 per cent. Now who the hell knew which it was?

'But I'll tell you what. When a top police official in

Holland acknowledges that 40, 50 per cent of the people in that Red Light District are in slavery, then we've got a problem here. Can you imagine if in any country you had a district where you were allowed to manufacture widgets and it was a slavery district where 50 per cent of the people were enslaved?'

Miller's righteous anger – the same anger inside me and the same anger I hope you feel – paid off, just a little bit. As we saw for ourselves, Dutch officials can now provide an accurate figure for the percentage of prostitutes who are sex slaves – 80 per cent. That's the good news. The bad news is that the number is obviously rising: 50 per cent when John Miller visited Amsterdam a decade ago, 80 per cent today. But he faced a huge problem: everyone is against slavery, but no one can agree on how to stop it.

Take the United Nations as an example. There's a UN law outlawing slavery but the UN operates by consensus: the lowest common denominator wins out.[1] So what happens? They agree on the United Nations protocol that is against slavery but they leave every nation to enforce it. And different countries – as we shall see – enforce different bits, in different ways. This, as John Miller saw for himself, isn't about some abstract idea or boring policy discussion: it's about whether women like me are protected from sex-slavers. And if they're not, it's meant to make sure we are found and released from the Hell we're in. And for me, read Cristina, Natalya and Katya. Or Susanna, or Mardea or any of the thousands upon thousands of women like us who are tricked by traffickers and sold to vicious criminals, who make money from our suffering bodies. No, this isn't boring: it's vital.

So what did John Miller do? He fought, that's what.

Every year the United States government publishes a huge document called the 'Trafficking In Persons' report. It assesses what every country – and I mean *every* country – in the world does to stop slavery. Each country has to submit information to Washington DC to describe the number of cases it prosecuted, the outcomes of those trials, the number of women (and men and children) rescued from slavery and what it is doing to help them once they have been freed.

Each country is graded – just as in an annual school report: Tier 1 countries are the ones judged to be fully complying with their legal obligations to tackle slavery; Tier 2 is the equivalent of the report I used to get from my teacher – 'could do better'. And Tier 3 is reserved for countries that aren't doing very much at all – the ones sitting at the back of the class, asleep.

It's a sort of global 'name and shame' report, but it's also got teeth. America doles out vast sums in aid money to countries all across the world – more than $52 billion a year. Countries with a Tier 3 rating risk being excluded from a share of that money and can have economic sanctions taken against them.

And John Miller, who fought so hard for the TIP Report to carry this big stick, found it made a difference. 'That was my job and not just banging heads with diplomats, or confronting government officials, talking with the police, or working at rehabilitation centres and looking at the prevention education programmes. I found that while people of course would resent US interference, in the case of government officials I found that the shame that was caused by being ranked in Tier 2 or Tier 3 was very influential.

'And if the United States or I as the ambassador said: "Look, here's how you can improve and raise your rating or here's how it will go down and the world will see what'll happen and you may even be exposed to sanctions under US law," this really had some impact.'

So that's all alright, then? I wish it was.

Let's look at what the latest TIP says about some of the countries we've been to, starting with the Netherlands.

The Netherlands is a source, destination and transit country for men, women and children subjected to trafficking in persons, specifically forced prostitution and forced labour. The Netherlands, Nigeria, Hungary, Bulgaria, Poland, Guinea, Romania and China are the top eight countries of origin for identified victims of mostly forced prostitution, according to the government, although victims from Macedonia and Uganda were also found. Often criminal networks are involved in forced prostitution and forced labour involving foreigners.

The Netherlands prohibits all forms of trafficking through criminal code Article 273, which prescribes maximum sentences ranging from eight to 18 years' imprisonment. In 2010, the last year for which final trafficking statistics were available, the government prosecuted 135 suspected trafficking offenders, convicting 107 – a significant increase from the 69 offenders convicted in 2009.

The average sentence for convicted trafficking offenders was approximately 21 months. In accordance with the law, convicted offenders generally serve only two-thirds of their sentences, suggesting that many convicted trafficking offenders likely serve little more than a year in jail. Local police complain that low sentences for traffickers continued to result in the reappearance of the same offenders and thus the continued exploitation of trafficking victims within the regulated commercial sex sector.

Now tell me, if your child came home with a school report like that would you think it was good or bad? Would you think it merited a prize or a punishment – or something in between? I know what I think – and John Miller thinks so, too. 'I was in Amsterdam, I was in the Hague; I met with professionals, I met with the government, I even met with the news media. And er, I have to say that some battles I won, some I lost. And I lost this one. Holland was given Tier 1 status – the best there is.

'I didn't believe the Netherlands was Tier 1. I thought what went on in the Red Light Districts was slavery. Just by itself that meant they couldn't be rated Tier 1. But I lost the case. The deputy secretary of our State department in Washington said: "Well, let's make Tier 1 conditional and we'll send you over to Holland to meet with Dutch officials and tell 'em if they don't do better, they'll be downgraded."

'And so I went over there and I met with them, and they

did maybe a few things but not much, and they stayed in Tier 1. You know, all I can say is I didn't think according to our law that they were Tier 1, but there they are.'

Does this matter? Isn't this some meaningless piece of international diplomacy that doesn't actually make any difference? No, it isn't. It's about women like me. And it's about the people who make money from us being forced to lie on our backs and let men invade our bodies. It matters. Oh God, it matters. But don't take my word for it: listen to Lodewijk Asscher, deputy mayor of Amsterdam and the politician with overall responsibility for Amsterdam's Red Light District.

'We have to abandon our romantic view of the Red Light District. Hard-line criminal behaviour is what is happening behind those windows, women subjected to extremes of exploitation. They have a non-existent debt they have to pay to a pimp by prostituting themselves. They are physically abused if they don't work hard enough.

'It's very difficult to tackle effectively. Very frustrating for the police and the courts. The penalties are often minor; there is also an absence of public indignation. Recently we were dealing with a pimp who had used violent methods to force 110 women into work. The only sign of public anger was when the man escaped.

'This is our last chance. Prostitution has been legal for 10 years now. We have to clamp down hard on these abusers. After all, slavery was abolished a long time ago in the Netherlands.'

Fine words, and amen to every single one of them. But what is the Netherlands actually doing? It's not getting rid of its legal prostitution industry – even though it knows that this is what causes women like me to be trafficked there. No, it is planning to 'regulate it just that bit more carefully'. Tell me, wasn't John Miller right to say that this is just like the Dutch policy of giving slaves slightly better treatment, 250 years ago?

Maybe if Holland wasn't the only battle Miller had lost then it wouldn't be so bad but take a look at the TIP Report – you can because it's on the Internet for everyone to see. In the report, every country that has legalised prostitution is accused of being a place where women are trafficked and sold into the sex industry: every single one. And yet every one of them gets a Tier 1 rating.

Now, let's go back to the first country we visited, you and I. Let's return to Moldova, poor impoverished Moldova, whose women are the most highly-prized in brothels around the world: the country which has the biggest proportion of its women trafficked into international sex slavery.

In the summer of 2012, the parliament in Moldova began considering a new law: a law that would make it illegal for anyone to purchase sexual services. Think about that: instead of a law which punishes a woman for being a prostitute, this law would punish the men whose selfish lusts brought her to a brothel in the first place. That's a good law, isn't it? Doesn't that deserve a Gold Star from the US government?

TIP REPORT 2012: MOLDOVA. TIER 2
Moldova is a source and, to a lesser extent, a transit and destination country for women and girls

subjected to sex trafficking. Moldovan women are subjected to forced prostitution in Turkey, Russia, Cyprus, the United Arab Emirates (UAE), Bulgaria, Kosovo, Israel, Indonesia, Malaysia, Lebanon, Italy, Greece, Ukraine, the Czech Republic, Romania, Poland, Slovenia, Spain, Tajikistan and Ukraine.

The Government of Moldova does not fully comply with the minimum standards for the elimination of trafficking; however, it is making significant efforts to do so.

The government has made progress over the past year in addressing the protection of victims and the prevention of trafficking.

However, the government did not show sufficient progress in addressing widespread complicity in trafficking by law enforcement and other public officials. Reports of widespread corruption in the police and judicial system persisted and no officials were convicted for trafficking-related offences.

Furthermore, despite increased prosecutions in comparison to the previous year, the number of convictions declined and the proportion of convicted offenders receiving prison sentences declined as well. The government provided inadequate witness protection for some victims waiting to testify in court.

Stop. Stop right there. You remember Alexandr 'Salun' Kovali – the Moldovan sex trafficker who, as I write this, is locked up in a tiny, dirty cell in a shabby, rusting prison? And you remember Saban Baran – the violent sex trafficker sunning himself on the beach in Antalya after Dutch officials let him out of prison? Just who do you think is 'complying with minimum standards'; just who is 'showing sufficient progress'?

Tell you what: let's ask the people in Moldova who devote their lives to working with trafficked women. Let's ask Ana Revenco.

'Very often we see that economically strong countries are always making good in this Report – although these are the countries where our citizens are exploited. These are the countries which fail to recognise our women as victims, as women who were violated.

'These are the countries that failed to ensure protection for our women; these are the countries that have double standards. And yet they are rewarded.'

I couldn't agree more.

But just before we leave Moldova, there's something else in that TIP Report: '[Moldovan] Government complicity in human trafficking remained a significant concern and no government officials were convicted for trafficking-related complicity in 2011.'

Looks bad, doesn't it? That's enough to get Moldova a poor grade, enough to push it ever nearer to economic sanctions. Except consider this.

There are more than 1,200 prostitution businesses throughout Holland today: Amsterdam alone has 300 brothels, prostitution earns the government of the Netherlands €660 million every year. Four million tourists flock to Amsterdam – most of them coming to stare at and often 'patronise' the prostitutes working in its neon-lit windows. Amsterdam City Council reaps €83 million from that tourist windfall, even though its own statistics show that 80 per cent – at least – of those prostitutes have been trafficked. Now doesn't that make the Dutch government 'complicit' in human trafficking? Worse still, doesn't this mean that it is knowingly profiting from it?

And now ask yourself: how much of that money does the Netherlands pour back into helping dirt-poor countries like Moldova stop the export of its women? If you want to know the reality, ask Ion Vizdoga: 'Moldova has neither the resources nor the infrastructure to stop the trafficking of its women into sex slavery. But the problem is not about Moldova. In fact, the problem is about the countries where these victims are exploited. Those countries' societies have a problem, if men exploit helpless girls and women – women who are forced to accept prostitution in order to just support their families from Moldova, a very poor country.'

And what about us? How does Britain come out of the slavery report? Here's what it says about us:

> The United Kingdom (UK) is a destination country for men, women, and children primarily from Africa, Asia, and Eastern Europe who are subjected to sex trafficking and forced labour, including domestic servitude. According to the Crown Prosecution Service, between April and December 2011, the British government prosecuted 87 offences of trafficking for sexual exploitation.
>
> The government did not provide comprehensive sentencing data for convicted trafficking offenders in

2011; however, the government reported the average penalty for convicted trafficking offenders in 2011 was 27.2 months' imprisonment.

That's 87 prosecutions. An average jail sentence of two-and-a-half years. Is this the same country which according to the *Guardian* newspaper is in the midst of a 'moral panic' over a non-existent problem? But more to the point, how do we rate in the way we treat women who have been trafficked, women like Katya? Has Britain, as the government promised we would do after that case, made sure we protect them better? Have a guess.

In July 2011, the UK government adopted a new government strategy on trafficking. Some anti-trafficking experts in the UK criticised the strategy for its emphasis on border control. These experts report that their limited role in formal victim identification leads to trafficking victims not being recognised as such and thus criminalised or deported without access to assistance. NGOs criticised a narrow focus on victims' immigration status, reporting that as a result, EU nationals were more likely to receive a 'positive grounds conclusion' or otherwise be officially recognised as trafficking victims by UK authorities.

Anti-trafficking experts continued to report that many other victims were not referred through the National Reporting Mechanism, as victims do not see the benefits of referral, are afraid of retribution

OF ANGELS AND PINS

by their traffickers, or fearful of the consequences of being brought to the attention of authorities because of their immigration status. Anti-trafficking experts cited ongoing concerns regarding implementation of this mechanism, resulting in unidentified and identified victims being detained, punished or deported.

In other words, nothing has really changed. And yet Britain gets a pat on the back and Tier 1 status. Are you surprised that I'm angry?

It's not as if we can't see the problem. It's not that sex-trafficked women are invisible or somehow hidden away in some remote and inaccessible part of the country. Do something for me: pick up your local paper and study the adverts section at the back. Straight away you'll come face to face with sex slaves. Spotted them yet? Maybe this will help.

It's a letter sent to newspaper editors by the head of Scotland Yard's anti-trafficking team.

Dear Editor,
As you will be aware, the Metropolitan Police Service is committed to reducing human trafficking and sexual exploitation. Recent investigations have demonstrated our commitment to ensuring London remains a hostile environment to those engaged in this type of criminality and a number of these investigations have resulted in successful prosecutions.

It is clear from a considerable number of these operations that advertising in newspapers can play a key role in facilitating the exploitation of trafficked victims. The adverts in question often purport to be massage parlours, saunas or escort agencies, but are in reality a front for criminal networks to advertise trafficked victims for sexual services. Consequently it is vital that we tackle this area as part of our over-arching strategy to reduce trafficking in London.

I am therefore seeking your support to help us address this issue by ensuring that your publications do not allow advertising space to be utilised to promote these practices. Advertisements that offer multi-national or young women; or which are sexually suggestive in tone are often the type found to be linked to the provision of sexual services and/or the presence of trafficked women.

It is these types of adverts I am seeking your support in preventing. I would ask that you put in place a system to satisfy yourselves that those seeking to place advertisements are genuine concerns or businesses and not a cover for the types of criminal activity high-lighted above.

As you will appreciate, criminal liability can arise in certain circumstances where evidence clearly shows that the advertising in question supports or promotes offences associated to trafficking, exploitation or proceeds of crime.

Richard Martin, Detective Chief
Superintendent, OCU Commander SCD9
Human Exploitation and Organised Crime Unit

Now can you see the trafficked women? They're for sale in your local paper.

If you doubt this, perhaps you should meet Sergei Konart and Ekaterina Kolesikova. In October 2011 they were jailed for a total of 12 years after pleading guilty to a series of charges, including trafficking and controlling prostitution.

Konart and Kolesikova belonged to a Russian and European-based organised criminal network. They recruited at least 13 vulnerable young Eastern European women to come to the UK by promising them opportunities to make large amounts of money as waitresses, shop assistants or dancers. But once the women arrived in Britain, Konart and Kolesikova took their victim's identity and travel documents. They then told each girl she owed them up to £80,000. And of course there were no nice safe jobs in cafés or shops: instead these terrified women were forced into prostitution in brothels and 'massage parlours' in Chelsea, Kensington and Earls Court. If they refused, they were beaten and then drugged with ecstasy and cocaine to make them compliant.

Hanna Llewellyn-Waters, the barrister prosecuting Konart and Kolesikova, told Southwark Crown Court that their victims were told they could only leave if they paid off tens of thousands of pounds of their 'debts'. 'These women were effectively enslaved by a debt bondage into working as prostitutes at the defendants' behest. Threats were made to their families and there were concerns they might be targeted by the criminal network in Russia.'

In her witness account, given in open court, one of the victims said the work she was being forced to do 'made her skin crawl'. She said she felt 'sick' because lots of the clients were 'disgusting'. She 'hated' her life and knew that it was very harmful for her health and was having a big impact on her mental state. Another victim told the court: 'I felt used and thrown away.'

Now where do you think all the men who used and abused these young women found out about the brothels? Local advertising, that's how. Speaking after their sentences were handed down, Detective Inspector Kevin Hyland from the SCD9 Human Exploitation and Trafficking Unit had a message for such 'clients': 'Traffickers have no regard for the rights or well-being of those they exploit. Anyone who uses prostitution services needs to be aware that they are part of the exploitation and may be committing offences.'

Let me ask you something. If I bought space for an advert in a newspaper asking for people to come and commit a crime – and hundreds or even thousands did so – do you think that the newspaper would be committing? After all, it profited from the crime without ever having to get its hands dirty. But newspapers up and down the country still rake in the cash from adverts for 'massage parlours', 'saunas' and 'escort services' – all these are euphemisms for prostitution. And time after time we find out that behind these weasel words there are sex slaves, trafficked and traded into their own personal Hell.

As far as I know only one newspaper group has taken a stand and refused to carry any more of these adverts. And the rest? They're happy to take the money and turn a blind eye.

We know prostitution exists, we know that it sometimes

often, apparently involves sex trafficking and slavery yet we, as a country, as a society, seem to have come to accept that it's just a normal, acceptable part of our way of life. Perhaps we just don't care enough about these women – women like me. Perhaps they are, perhaps I am, the 'wrong' kind of victim.

And perhaps that's why I wasn't at all surprised when I picked up my local newspaper and read the latest sex-trafficking story: this one was close to home, in Newcastle just a few miles up the road.

You don't get much more central than Pilgrim Street. It's smack in the middle of the city on a direct route from the Tyne Bridge. It boasts two cinemas, a listed 18th-century merchant's house and it's at the heart of a massive regeneration project. Until June 2011, it also had a brothel.

But it didn't call itself that – of course it didn't. It called itself a 'medical centre' and advertised massages, Chinese Viagra and treatments to boost sex drive in its window. But what really happened behind that window?

Just after 11am on Wednesday, 8 June, uniformed and plain-clothes officers from Northumbria Police and the UK Border Agency pushed through crowds of shoppers and marched inside. When they emerged, they brought out people in handcuffs and two women of Chinese origin.

A statement, by Andy Radcliffe of the UK Border Agency was issued to the press: 'Today's operation follows an investigation into the suspected trafficking of foreign nationals into the UK sex trade.'

Why am I telling you this? Why, when we have been halfway round the world, investigated vicious international trafficking gangs and met the sorrowful victims of sex slavery; why am I bothered about a raid on a small suspected brothel in the middle of the city centre? Surely it's just another sad – if mundane – shabby example? Surely it just goes to show that we are actually doing something about this; that the police do actually stop alleged sex traffickers?

How I wish that were true. But there are two things I need to tell you about that suspected brothel in the heart of Newcastle upon Tyne. The first is that it was hidden – if that's the word – in plain sight: not just of you and I, but of the very people who are meant to stop this happening. It was less than 100 yards from a police station.

And the second? Oh, that's worse; much, much worse.

One of the people charged and presently awaiting trial for running this little corner of Hell is a police officer.

---

[1] The Palermo Protocols, passed in 2000, set out to prevent trafficking in people – especially women and children.

CHAPTER TEN

THE ELEPHANT IN THE ROOM

Home. I am home. The colours on the hills I can see from my window are fading to dull winter brown. The fire is on, the room is warm and safe; a cup of milky coffee steams on the table by my chair.

We have been on a long journey, you and I. We have seen much and met many people. We have heard their stories – harrowing, painful accounts of abuse and re-abuse, remarkably similar to the story you shared of my life. Thank you. Thank you for coming this far with me.

But we are not alone. There is something in this room with us – something too big to ignore. We have to face it, just as we have had to face all the pain and hurt on our travels.

Do you remember the story *The Elephant and The Blind Men*? I think now we – you, me, all of us – have finally taken off our blindfolds. We can see the elephant for what it is, not what we might have thought – or wanted to think – when each of us only felt a little part of it. It is an elephant. And it is in this room, here with us. Now that we've recognised it we have to face it.

The elephant has a name – and its name is prostitution.

Sooner or later, all arguments about how to stop sex trafficking and sex slavery bump, uncomfortably, into this elephant. One side of the argument – and it is an argument, no question about that – says the only way to stop women being tricked and trafficked into sex slavery is to legalise and regulate prostitution. Once selling sex is taken away from the threat of prosecution, women will be able to choose whether to be prostitutes, free from the pressure of pimps and violent criminals. The other side argues that only by making it illegal for men (or women, come to that) to pay for sex, can we rid ourselves of the sex-slavers who trade in women's bodies.

This is the elephant – and we need to talk about it.

But first, I want to ask you a question. Can you remember the names of all the people who you have ever had sex with? I'll bet that most of you can. But I can't. Because with very, very few exceptions I never knew them: the men who took pleasure from my body never told me their names. And now, another question: Does this matter? Think about it for a moment and tell me: in your own lives, if you never knew even the name of the person who touched and entered you – much less anything about their lives, their hopes, their dreams, their beliefs, their history – would it matter to you?

We'll come back to this, you and I. But first, we should hear from men who use prostitutes. If we want to know why a real elephant sometimes gets out of control, if we want to understand how and why it moves and what makes it stop, we would need to hear from the person who controls it: the man sitting on its back, who drives it from one task to the next. In the case of our 'elephant', it's the customers: the 'clients', 'punters' or 'johns'. What is it that makes men pay for sex – and what do they believe about the women whose bodies they rent?

For years, people have asked the same questions. Academic studies pop up from time to time, based around interviews with anonymous (of course) men, who admit to paying for sex. And each time, in each piece of research, the same answers crop up again and again.

'Prostitution is like masturbating without having to use your hand.'

'It's like renting a girlfriend or wife. You get to choose, like a catalogue.'

'No big deal, it's just like getting a beer.'

'My favourite experience in prostitution was when she was totally submissive.'

'I don't like the ones that make no secret of it being a job – I like customer care. They try to finish quickly, but I want to take a little bit of time.'

'I have sex as a means to an end to meet my sexual needs. It's a financial transaction.'

'Lots of men go to prostitutes so they can do things to them that real women would not put up with.'

'If you go to the wrong one, you might as well be in a morgue – there's a slab of flesh there.'
'We're living in the age of instant coffee, instant food: this is instant sex.'
'Prostitution is a last resort to unfulfilled sexual desires.'
'Prostitution is like being able to masturbate without doing any of the work.'
'You pay for the convenience, a bit like going to a public loo'.[1]

Tell me, when you have sex do you think of it as just another form of masturbation? Does it feel like 'going to the loo' or making 'instant coffee'? I ask you because in one sense I'm the wrong person to give an answer. I have been penetrated by hundreds of men but I never chose any of them so my outlook is pretty much guaranteed to be slightly jaundiced, but you – you have normal lives that don't involve having guns pointed at your heads, lives that won't spiral down into the despair of drugs and drink. Do those descriptions match your experience of sex in any way at all?

No? Well, that's what men who pay for sex actually think. Here's another one: this is what he himself posted on a highly respectable, internationally organised online debate forum.[2]

I do not understand the real difference between prostitution and dating. Both involve sex, often willingly and sometimes reluctantly, but prostitution is different from rape. What distinguishes prostitution is the money transaction. Well, money is involved in all kinds of work. Almost all of us sell our body to make a living. Prostitution is not that romantic, neither is dating. More often than not, dating is rather awkward. Prostitution has one advantage: it is fair and efficient. Both agree to a price and a period. This is no different from going to a McDonald's to get a hamburger during lunch break.

Like I say, my experiences may make my opinions a bit skewed. But I have been on both sides of this equation: I've been on dates and I've been a prostitute. So let me tell you the difference.

When I've gone on a date – or even had a one-night stand – I've sometimes had sex. But that sex has happened because both of us are attracted to each other and we have *wanted* to have sex. It hasn't been because my date has paid for dinner or given me anything: no money has exchanged hands, unless you count maybe paying for my share of the meal or the taxi afterwards (and no, that doesn't count).

On a date, sex is not a transaction. It's a mutual decision by two adult people who happen to want to enjoy pleasure together.

Having sex with a prostitute works like this – or at least it did in my case. Man walks up and down the street. Man wants to have an orgasm. Man cruises past the available women until he picks one. Man goes to his chosen prostitute and asks how much. He might ask whether there are any 'extras' (anal, bondage, a little rough stuff?) and how much each will cost.

A price is agreed; a transaction entered into. There will probably be noises coming from nearby rooms, but the man either won't notice or care. He may try to speak to 'his' prostitute but when he finds she doesn't speak his language, he just gets on with taking his pleasure. He instructs the woman what he wants her to do – suck this, bend over there, let me come on your breasts. When he has finished, he puts on his clothes, zips up his flies and walks out. He doesn't see, hear or think about what that woman saw, heard or felt.

Now can someone tell me what are the similarities between a date and using a prostitute? Where are we going with all of this? Simple: there is one reason and one reason alone why men pay for sex. Because they can. And there's one simple reason why women sell their bodies: because they have to. Men make a choice, women face a choice.

That choice can sometimes – sometimes – be economic. A choice between getting enough food, often for a young family, or going without. Take a look through all the hundreds of stories published by women who have sold sex.

You'll find that the ones like 'Belle de Jour' who sold her enormously successful blog to a television company as the basis for a 'drama' about the wonderful life of a high-class call girl are in a tiny, tiny minority. Most say that they let men rent their bodies because it was the only way to make enough money to live. And then read what they say about the price of prostitution. No, not the money they charged or made – even if they got to keep any of it – but the price they paid.

I came across one such blog at the end of my journey. It's the story of a young woman who was an escort for more than four years.[3] Listen to what she has to say.

I am not making any excuses for punters here, and I'm not apologising for their behaviour and attitudes towards women. Neither am I vilifying all punters as violent sexual deviants. It doesn't make what they do okay, just because some of them are nice about it. Getting mugged is getting mugged, whether the mugger is polite to you or not. You've still just been mugged.

In a way I wish that all punters were violent and abusive to me. That would be much easier to get over. Clear-cut things are always much easier to get over. Why do you think things like long-term sexual abuse are so hard to deal with? Because it's abuse disguised as normalcy. I was sexually abused until 7 years ago, but I've only seen it clearly for what it was a few months ago.

I've gotten over the punter who tried to rape me, who shoved my head into the ground and used his entire upper body weight to keep me there so that I couldn't breathe or speak. I've gotten over the guy who held my hair in a vice grip and forced me to deepthroat him. Sometimes he lifted my face off his dick before shoving it with a strength I've never experienced before back onto his dick (this was all the while saying how 'beautiful' I was).

I've gotten over the middle-aged man, when I first started, who did not say one word to me for the entire encounter, and who had a thick crusty ring around his dick, which of course I sucked. I've gotten over the guy who threw his money at me while pressuring me to do more 'favourites'. I've gotten over the punter laughing at my cum-covered face after a gang bang. He laughed at me in a joking way. I guess I was supposed to also find it funny. I wonder how funny he would've found it, though. I've gotten over the S&M punter who threatened to use a bigger 'device' if I complained about the smaller one (I've also gotten over him trying to inadvertently be my pimp). These are real-life punters, not one-off experiences. They think that they are normal guys. They think that they can pull my hair or force me to deepthroat just because they paid me to accept it. Paying takes away any responsibility towards me as a human being.

I felt like a tool. I felt like a piece of equipment. And that's it.

The nicer punters hurt me but they didn't know it. Remember what I said about being a great actress and a master manipulator? I wanted them to believe that I was happy. I was adamant that this was what I wanted to be doing. As long as no one ever questioned me on that, I was fine – I was emotionally surviving. I know it seems really idealistic but I wish a punter had asked me why I was doing it, or what led me there, and I would have had an emotional breakdown and all this might already be behind me, but thinking like that is just immature. Punters aren't stupid. Some can see past the strongest facades. They just choose not to acknowledge it as then, I'm guessing, they'd have to look inwards as well.

Punters either knowingly or unknowingly hurt me, and hurt themselves. They had a big (huge) hand to play in what I am going through now, and I firmly believe that most punters are not happy people, or don't know what real happiness is to compare.

I think that that the easy availability of sex and the normalising effect that escort websites have distorts the truth massively for many, many people involved, and I was one of those people.

I hope this young woman doesn't mind me reprinting that here. I don't think she will because in the introduction to her blog, she says: 'This is where I have a voice; this is where I can say the truth... thank you for reading. I appreciate it more than I can say.'

Go and read what she has to say. Do it now and then we can put to bed, once and for all, the myth of the happy hooker.

Oh, but you say: I've read plenty of quotes in the newspapers from women who say they have chosen this 'profession'. And yes – yes, you have. Here's one, from Cari Mitchell, a mother and grandmother and a state-registered nurse, as well as a spokeswoman for the English Collective of Prostitutes (http://prostitutescollective.net): 'Most sex workers are single mothers and many go into prostitution because of poverty, domestic violence, homelessness and debt. Women can leave sex work if they want but what prevents them is a criminal record. A conviction prohibits them from getting an alternative job, especially if they want to work with children.'

What, or who, is the English Collective of Prostitutes? Read on.

The English Collective of Prostitutes (ECP) and the US PROStitutes Collective (US PROS) are part of the International Prostitutes Collective. We are in touch with sex workers all over the world.

The situation of those of us in Third World countries and those of us who work the streets, often Black women, other women of colour and/or immigrant women, has always been our starting point.

Since 1975, the International Prostitutes Collective has been campaigning for the abolition of the prostitution laws which criminalize sex workers and our families, and for economic alternatives and higher benefits and wages.

No woman, child or man should be forced by poverty or violence into sex with anyone. We provide information, help and support to individual prostitute women and others who are concerned with sex workers' human, civil, legal and economic rights.

Now when you put it like that, it all seems to make sense, doesn't it? After all, we own our bodies, don't we? And if we choose to rent parts of them to men, well then that's our choice and no government or police officer should get in the way of us earning a living. Right?

Wrong.

Because the truth is that – despite what the ECP and US PROS say – most prostitutes don't have the option of leaving. The truth is that most prostitutes are being forced to sell sex by someone else.

Don't misunderstand me. I don't believe that prostitutes

– men or women – should be regarded as criminals. What I do believe – what I know as a stone-cold fact – is that women should not be forced to be sex slaves. Which means that we need to find the best way to stop sex trafficking: to stop women like me, like Cristina, Natalia, Katya, Mardea, Susanna and all those unnamed human beings whose bodies are traded like commodities by greedy, selfish traffickers, and to protect them.

This isn't a moral question. It's a question of hard, practical realities.

Now, there are plenty of people who argue that the way to stop sex trafficking is to legalise prostitution. Some states in Australia have adopted a system of legalisation coupled with licensing and claim that it works very well.

> There is no doubt that licensed brothels provide the safest working environment for sex workers in Queensland. The legal brothels provide a sustainable model for a healthy, crime-free, and safe legal licensed brothel industry and are a state of the art model for the sex industry in Australia.[4]

That sounds good, doesn't it? Safe, healthy and crime-free... Except that it isn't. Two of the states that have adopted a legalised prostitution industry have already reported serious problems with crime and regulation.

In August 2010, a fire at a brothel in South Melbourne initially thought to have been started by a defective fan heater turned into something altogether more worrying when police uncovered allegations of a turf war between proprietors of the city's legalised brothels. A year-long investigation by the State of Victoria revealed that brothels were permitted to renew licences despite an accumulation of police intelligence – documented criminal activity which included a killing and other suspected fire bombings. What's worse, police raids have found numerous sex-trafficking victims working in legalised establishments. And, despite legalisation, illegal brothel syndicates run by organised crime gangs have flourished.

And it's not just Australia. There are 61 countries in the world that have either completely legalised prostitution industries or have a semi-legalised approach of tolerance without actually making the purchase of sex illegal. With the exception of three of those countries – Bangladesh, Bolivia and Uruguay – sex trafficking is endemic. How do I know? Because that American government country-by-country Trafficking In Persons report starts with exactly this phrase for each of them: 'a source, transit, and destination country for men, women, and children subjected to sex trafficking and forced labour'.

I don't know what that says to you, but it tells me that legalising prostitution doesn't stop sex trafficking.

At the same time, even the countries where all forms of prostitution are illegal are not immune from sex trafficking. But let's look again at that TIP Report and at one country in particular: Sweden.

In 1999, the Swedish Parliament passed a new and radical law which made it a criminal offence to buy sexual services while legally treating the woman as a victim. Pimping, procuring and operating a brothel were also made illegal, but what was completely new was the idea of criminalising the demand for prostitution, not the supply. In other words, instead of turning women who were forced – either by trafficking or poverty – to sell sex into criminals, men who chose of their own free will to pay to use women's bodies risked prosecution.

The Swedish government also established a comprehensive outreach programme that encourages sex workers to change their livelihood and made absolutely clear that the reason behind this new law was the dangers prostitution posed to women and to society as a whole.

> Prostitution is considered to cause serious harm both to individuals and to society as a whole. Large-scale crime, including human trafficking for sexual purposes, assault, procuring and drug-dealing, is also commonly associated with prostitution. (...)The vast majority of those in prostitution also have very difficult social circumstances.

Guess what happened next?

In 1995, a Swedish government commission estimated that there were 2,500–3,000 women in prostitution throughout the country; 650 of them worked on the streets. Thirteen years later – after nearly 10 years of prostitution being completely illegal – Sweden had just 300 street prostitutes, and around the same number who worked in clandestine brothels or in private flats.

The same research showed that the percentage of men purchasing anyone for prostitution had decreased from

13.6 per cent in 1996 to 8 per cent in 2008 – a drop of nearly 50 per cent. Swedish Detective Superintendent Jonas Trolle rammed the point home: 'We have decreased the number of customers radically. If we talk in specific figures of the number of girls or women in prostitution in Stockholm, on a street level there are between five and 10 girls a day in a city with over five million people.'

The research concludes that law functions as a barrier against bringing in 'foreign women' for prostitution and cuts down on organised crime networks in Sweden. And what did the 2012 TIP Report show? That sex trafficking is on the wane, that's what.

> Although in previous years forced prostitution has been the dominant type of trafficking in Sweden, in 2011 the number of reported labour trafficking victims was larger than the number of reported sex trafficking victims.

Compare this to the Netherlands and Germany – both of whom have led the charge for legal prostitution. We've already met, you and I, the women tricked and trafficked into the Red Light Districts; we've also seen first hand the ease with which vicious international criminals can sell women's unwilling bodies in the country's legal sex industry.

We've already heard that most estimates suggest at least 80 per cent of the prostitutes working in Holland are from other countries – and that they're selling sex because someone is forcing them to. And guess what's happened to the number of women proven – proven – to have been trafficked into the Netherlands? It's going up and up and up each year. CoMensha (www.mensenhandel.nl.cms) – the national anti-trafficking organisation headed up by Jerrol Martens registered 1,222 trafficking victims in 2011 – an increase from 993 victims registered in 2010 and a consistent increase from previous years.

And what about Germany, with its clinically efficient legalised prostitution zones and licensed brothels? The federal government in Berlin announced that human trafficking increased by 70 per cent between 2005 and 2010, and another 11 per cent between 2009 and 2010. Most of those proven – that word again, proven – cases involved women forced into prostitution. Just like the Netherlands, while Germany legalised prostitution to end criminal involvement in the market, the number of organised crime groups running prostitution there has also increased.

Marianne Eriksson, a Swedish member of the European Parliament and a strong proponent of her country's legal strategy on sex trafficking, sums it up this way: 'What differentiates us from the Netherlands and Germany is that we link the "slave trade" with prostitution. Everyone in the European Union is against human trafficking, of course, but we know that 90 percent of this commerce has to do with sexual exploitation. Our method reduces this.'

Still not convinced? Try this: a highly scientific study of 150 countries with widely differing laws on prostitution – from the legal Red Lights of Australia, German and the Netherlands through the 'Amber Lights' of countries like

Britain, which turn a largely blind eye to the determined, hard-line nations which completely forbid the purchase of sex.[5] It's chock-full of incredibly intricate statistical equations, taking into account all the various factors, effects and conditions surrounding prostitution. And here's what all that mind-bogglingly scientific research boils down to: 'We find that countries with legalized prostitution have a statistically significantly larger reported incidence of human trafficking inflows.'

I've got a much simpler way of putting it: pimps don't suddenly become nice guys just because prostitution is legal.

But while we're on the subject of 'science', let's take a look at the other widely used argument for legalising prostitution: that it reduces rape.

It appears that there's actually one only – just the one – formal research study on this, conducted by a man called Kirby R. Cundiff, PhD. Dr Cundiff is Associate Professor of Finance (interesting that, he's an academic dealing in money) at North-eastern State University in Oklahoma. In April, 2004 he published a working paper entitled 'Prostitution and Sex Crimes'. Here's what he said: 'It is estimated that if prostitution were legalized in the United States, the rape rate would decrease by roughly 25 per cent for a decrease of approximately 25,000 rapes per year. The analysis seems to support the hypothesis that the rape rate could be lowered if prostitution was more readily available. This would be accomplished in most countries by its legalization.'

After reading this, I didn't know whether to laugh or cry. I wanted to laugh – no, to pour scorn – on this report because it is pure theory. No actual evidence, just theory. And cry? Oh, yes. Because what Dr Cundiff was arguing was that nice ordinary women, with nice, ordinary lives can sleep safer in their beds because some other women are deliberately and legally told they must be commercially raped on their behalf.

It's an argument that says for the good of society at large there is an acceptable number of women who can be bought and sold like pieces of meat and then forced – by violence or poverty – to allow themselves to be abused. Shouldn't all of us be free from sexual exploitation? How can prostitution eliminate rape when it is itself bought by rape: the rape of women like me and all the others you have met in this book? The connection between rape and prostitution is that women are turned into objects for men's sexual use; they can either be bought or stolen.

So, we have our elephant. Do you see it clearly now? Are you able to acknowledge it, to describe it, to talk about it? I know I am, and here's what I know: there is no way to make prostitution 'a little bit better' any more than it is possible to make domestic violence 'a little bit better'. I've seen and suffered both: you can't make them a little less bad. We have to make it illegal for men – or women – to buy sex. Prostitution isn't the 'oldest profession' – it's the oldest form of slavery. We need to stop this. And we need to stop it now, right now.

---

[1] Source: 'Men Who Buy Sex'. A research study of 103 men who describe their use of trafficked and non-trafficked women in prostitution: Eaves (charity), 2009.

2 *The New York Times*: debate on the legalisation of prostitution.
3 *Secret Diary of a Dublin Call Girl*.
4 Assessment of legalised brothels, State Government of Queensland.
5 *Does Legalized Prostitution Increase Human Trafficking?* Cho, Dreher and Neumayer, 2012.

CHAPTER ELEVEN

LOVE

What is love?

I am 33 years old. I have been an adult – or at least have been in an adult world – for half of my life. I have been a child first loved, then abused. I have been a young woman tricked and then trafficked. I have been a prostitute and a drug addict. I have been a wife and a divorcee. I have been to Hell and come back. And this I know: the most important, the most essential and yet the most difficult challenge I have ever had to face is in that question. What is love?

It is almost Christmas. As I write this the nights have drawn short, the air is sharper and the wind more bitter. This, for me, is a time to think: to reflect on all that I have been and all that has been done to me. To sit quietly beside the fire, pen in one hand, a coffee in the other. Who is

Sarah Forsyth and how did she get here, to this warm, safe place? And how did you come to walk with her through this long journey? The answers are all in that question: what is love?

I think I used to dread Christmas. As a very young child it was a tough time. There was money in the good times but never enough in the bad; hardly surprising with a dad who ducked and dived, lived off his wits – and, all too often, off other people's money. Mum did so much to make it good for my brother, my little sister and me. She hid us from the pain of his beatings, even if she couldn't always conceal the bruises his fists left on her body. But even so we grew up with his callousness: to this day I remember the Christmas Eve he went to a pub to watch strippers and get drunk when he should have been building the dolls house which was supposed to be my little sister's present the next morning.

And then there was the abuse he inflicted on me. Hurting me, touching me in places a father should never touch a child, and making me touch and rub him until his pleasure came and it was over. Pushing himself – or knives or scissors – inside of me. Is this love? My dad would, I think, say that he loved me in his way. And if that way meant that he called me a bastard, claimed – quite wrongly – that I was someone else's child; if that love meant that he felt free to choke me with his beer fumes and his fag breath, before climbing under my bed covers and satisfying whatever needs he had – is that love? Can it be?

All of these memories. All of them come back, like photographic images flashing past my eyes.

LOVE

Mum: my poor, wonderful mum. Her face cut to ribbons from a milk bottle Dad had thrown at her; her lovely, pretty kind face needing stitches to put it back together again, then the scar covered with cosmetics so it wouldn't frighten us children. My parents loved each other – once. But what was that love? How can love live behind the veil of violence and abuse? And Christmas after Christmas: the best, the most precious, the most loving time of the year for a child. How can Christmas have any happiness when it is overshadowed?

A sip of coffee. Another memory. Sarah Forsyth is a teenager now: in a care home – a big, draughty mausoleum of a place in the countryside, miles from anywhere. Alone in a bunch of 25 other sullen and resentful kids – for children like us always hide our true selves behind the protective walls of hostility. Alone in a bed but not for long: a torch approaching through the dark, a beam of light in my eyes, a hand reaching for me. Fingers finding, probing, hurting my body: was that love – to him?

Care. Care home. In care... Meaningless words for no one cared, not really. No one in that cold, hard place would give us what we truly needed: love. Perhaps they couldn't, perhaps they never knew it.

A game. Children love games. Not this one, though. 'The Yellow Brick Road' – some weird, stupid adult's ritual. Crudely drawn roads and branch roads on a little piece of paper. Start on the main road, then choose your path: some are good, others bad. But none were paths of love. Hands grabbing me – again. Men – more than one – pinning me against a wall by my throat. Down, get down, you. Push, thrust, and a grunt of satisfaction. Was this some kind of love – to them? Does mere sexual release mean love? Can it ever?

Fast forward. A courtroom. Lawyers, experts, a judge. My dad, charged with the crimes he inflicted on me. And the last words he ever spoke to me: 'You little bastard – I'll kill you!' How can love grow when it has been sown in such a barren wasteland?

At 17 I learned a truth: I was pregnant.

Not a joyous pregnancy, a foetus borne of the love between two people. No, a dark and threatening swell in my belly, imperceptible except to me. A false move, a mistake by a girl who knew too much and too little all at the same time, and a man, an older man, who never knew.

Could I have loved this accident? Could I have raised a child – *my* child – and surrounded her (for it was a girl) with a warm and protective love? I shall never know. A car ride: Mum taking her daughter to a clinic to get rid of her granddaughter. The prick of a needle, the blissful smothering of anaesthetic and later the realisation of what I had lost. Sarah Forsyth: you destroyed the hope of life.

The wind has picked up. I hear it crying outside my window, blowing through my pleasant estate, house after house packed with families and children. I reach, automatically, to the table at my side: but no, they're not there. I no longer smoke. No cigarettes to support me as the memories reel past my eyes.

Another house, now. A front door to call my own and a man, too – a good man who knew all about me and what

252

had happened in my all-too short life. He knew about Dad, he knew about the abuse, he knew about the abortion. And he listened and held me and never judged. Oh, he was a good man, my Chris. And he loved me. There, I've said it – that word: love. Because he did love me and he treated me decently, and we had a home and holidays, and the makings of a happy life. And I couldn't take it.

I was wild then: headstrong, flirty and longing for the carefree life of a normal teenager. A life of clubs and excitement and laughter and silliness. But Chris was older than me; much older and more sedate. And so jealousy moved into our life, as my flirting drew appreciative looks from men much younger than him. Is jealousy part of love? How can it be when it eats away at the deepest foundations of a loving home?

A parting. No bitterness, no harsh words: just the slow, grinding realisation that it hadn't worked, that love – for us, as a couple – was over. Chris, if you're reading this: thank you. You brought love into my life and I'm so sorry that between us we killed it.

Talk to me: tell me, as you read this, do you know me yet? I sit here, in only the second real home I have ever known – at least if by 'home' we mean somewhere protected by the warmth of love – and I know that I must face these memories. I must look at the flickering images of my past if I am to make peace with the present. And especially if I am to have a future.

And so: Amsterdam. This is the most difficult, the most corrosive memory. Of course it is, you say; of course, we know what you went through, Sarah. We have been with you, we have supported you, we have cared. And yes, you have. But it's not what you think.

No one could ever mistake what John Reece – the man who trafficked me first – did for love. Greed, yes; and brutality and callousness and selfishness and pitiless calculation of what my body would be worth. But not love, not him.

And what goes for John Reece – wherever he is, assuming he is still alive and not killed by someone he cheated or conned or trafficked – goes for the men he sold me to.

Gregor and Pavel: I will never forget your faces, your harsh Yugoslav accents; your voices coldly telling me I had been bought and that I was now your property. I will never – can never – forget the women you enslaved with me or the dogs you set to guard us. I can see now the face of the frail and fearful Thai girl – poor, bewildered, trafficked Par – in that cold, dark place you took us to be filmed. I can see – frame by frame, as if in the slowest of slow-mo photography – the bullet shatter her skull and the pieces, the tiny, sticky fragments of her brain as they splashed on to me. No, no one could ever mistake what you did for love.

But what of the men who rented me? Could the awful, industrially organised business of prostitution have anything to do with love? Can a condom-covered 15-minutes of heaving and grinding ever do anything but mock true and honest love-making?

But there was love then. Oh yes, there was. And it has brought me nothing but trouble.

LOVE

You have come far with me on this journey; you know that Sally is not her name. I will not – would never – use her real name, for she has suffered enough and despite what she did to me I knew the flicker of true love with her.

You remember Sally: she was John Reece's accomplice. Another woman he used and abused, first by making her love him, then by prostituting her unwilling body to as many men as he could find to pay him. Then – oh yes, then – by getting her to bait the trap which would close around me.

It was Sally who posed as Reece's assistant; Sally who phoned to tell me the 'wonderful news' that I had passed my interview and got the job as a nursery nurse in Amsterdam. It was Sally who told me what my salary would be; Sally who made all the arrangements for my travel there; and it was Sally who met me at Schiphol airport and led me to the car, where John Reece put a gun to my head and told me there was no job in a crèche, just an existence as a sex slave behind the windows of the Red Light District. That was Sally, my Sally.

It was Sally who showed me what to do with the first man who paid to have sex with me. It was Sally who taught me the soul-sapping routine of posing and tantalising men who passed by our windows; Sally who warned me that if I didn't then Reece would beat the two of us black and blue.

It was Sally who introduced me to the drugs that would ease the pain of being raped a dozen times a day; Sally who gave me my first joint and my first line of coke that would finally lead me down the endless spiral of addiction.

Yes, all this Sally did to me. And I loved her. If truth be told, I think I love her still.

This, for some of you, is your stop: this is where you get off the train, abandon the journey. I know this: for in among the truly wonderful messages of support you sent me after I told you about all of this in my last book, in among the quiet whispers of encouragement which have seen me through some very dark moments; in and among these are those of you who say 'this cannot be – she cannot love this woman'.

I don't blame you. How could I? How, in the name of God, could anyone love the person who has played such a vital part in enslaving her – first as a prostitute, then as a crack whore? How? And you say – I know you do, for I have read what you have written – that either I have made some of this story up, or this was not – is not – a true love. And I don't blame you.

But it is true: all of it, every sad, sordid, miserable word. Every punch and every penetration; every loveless fuck and every entrapping inhalation – all of it is true. And so is the love I knew with Sally.

I don't ask you to understand – how could you? I don't expect you to see this as I saw it, to feel it as I felt it. All I ask is for you not to judge me – to accept that there are some things, there is some love, which can never appear rational. Do not judge me, please, for I have existed in a world where reason was subjugated to greed, where honesty was drowned in the pits of despair, and it was the same for Sally.

We two – we poor, brutalised, debased two – we clung

together. And in the very depths of Hell, we found some spark of humanity in each other. We found the quiet tenderness that needs no words, which somehow survives even the most bestial existence: we found love. And I know it still.

And then you say: well, even if we accept this absurd notion, how can this love have been good and true and wholesome? How, since you and Sally escaped from sex slavery and yet still went on to manage a brothel, how can you expect us to believe that this misshapen thing could be love?

Sometimes there is only one honest answer. I shall give it to you now: I don't know, I really don't know. I know that what Sally did to me has scarred me for life – I wear its pain indelibly and just beneath my skin. I know that the filthy midden of Amsterdam's Red Light District stained us for ever. I also know that what we did when we too profited from the abuse of other women is a self-inflicted wound that will rumble inside us until we die.

And yet. And yet she was my love, my true love. And the one who got away.

There. It is over. The slideshow of my past life has finished, the bright bulb of memory dimmed. We are close to the end of our journey. Now there is only the present – and a future.

I never thought I would write those last three words. At the end of my previous book I was sitting alone as I am sitting now, with a warm hot drink and a head full of memory. Of course I wanted a future but perhaps then I did not want it enough. Perhaps the vision of what could be – who I, Sarah Forsyth might yet be – was not clear enough. Perhaps that's why I remained locked in the past.

But now I see a future. I am clean of drugs and my body has not had to endure the poisons of alcohol or cigarettes for a long time. Hepatitis C has been vanquished. For the first time in my life, I am whole. I am still a young woman with a life to live and to enjoy.

There is, though, something I can never have. Something which I crave even more than I ever craved the drugs or the booze which controlled me. Something without which I can never be completely and utterly whole: a child.

It was Christmas two years ago when the idea began to take hold. Perhaps that was when I truly began to see the possibility of a future. It was the first Christmas I had spent with my family, all my family, except for Dad – who I never want to see and never will see again.

Mum came to pick me up on Christmas Eve and took me to Midnight Mass. I was nervous – when was the last time I had been in a church, when was the last time I had sat in the house of God and opened myself up to any judgement He might want to visit on me? But the church felt warm and loving. I didn't feel – as I feared I might – an outsider, an outcast, someone too dirty and damaged to be allowed inside.

And there was another reason for my anxiety: Rachel, my sister. All through the bleak years of my adult life we had been apart – separated by the vast, unbridgeable gulf of Amsterdam, my addiction and my appalling behaviour. Rachel, my precious sister, had kept her distance. It was a physical distance as well: Rachel has a wonderful job in America and rarely comes home. But Mum tells me now that she always asked about me even if she wasn't ready to see me. And now she was.

Christmas Day: a family day, with presents and good food. And above all a day with all the women in my life who love me still despite all that I have done, despite all that I have been: Gran, Mum and Rachel. It felt wonderful to be surrounded by their love and warmth and when Gran noticed that she and I were the only ones not drinking the champagne or the wine, she winked at me and said: 'Don't you worry. You and me will sit back and watch these getting drunk! Let's see who makes a fool of themselves first!' Thank you, Gran: you knew – you know – how much that meant to me.

And so, gradually, the thought began to grow in my mind. This is what love is: a quiet giving, with no thought of yourself, to someone who needs it. And who needs it more than a child?

My body, of course, was nowhere as advanced as my mind. Methadone still gripped it, Hepatitis C gnawed away inside it. But, as the months and the years passed and I finally took possession of my body – as I owned it, became responsible for it and allowed myself to love it – then the need to give love, unconditional and unfettered, took hold.

I spoke to my doctors and asked if I might be tested to see if my body could ever carry a child. With all that had been done to it, all that had been forced into it and with all the damage left by the drugs, this was the first big hurdle:

was I physically capable of conceiving? I wanted to hold my breath, but I didn't dare.

Tests: test after test after test. More probing and blood-taking and examination than I could ever imagine. But finally the news: yes, I was healthy – healthy enough to start new life in my belly and bring it, with love, into the world.

It took a day or so to sink in. Sarah Forsyth – ex crack whore – you can be fully a woman. Your body is strong enough. I knew then that I did have a future.

But how would I go about getting pregnant? One thing I knew for absolute certainty was that no man would ever penetrate me again. So many men have done so; so many times I have lain back, opened my legs and been taken. And never with love. Never. So how could I think of conceiving like this? I couldn't. No, I couldn't.

I am a gay woman. My only true romantic love is also my lost love. My mind still dreams sometimes of a home made with Sally – a home filled with love and caring... and children. But I know it's a dream, only a dream.

I spoke again to my doctors: now that I was officially fit enough to bear a child, could I be considered for IVF treatment? Might that be the way to allow me to bring new life to the world? Well, yes – and no.

I qualify for IVF – I am still young enough for the often-lengthy process to be viable. My sexuality is not an issue. But to be accepted by the NHS I would need to be in an established relationship: I would need to be one half of a couple.

My marriage to Tracy is long over and I don't think I

can ever be in a relationship again. How could I – honestly and truly – share my life with someone, when my heart, my love still belongs to Sally? I cannot deny that love and nor can I – will I ever – lie to another human being about my feelings. I have lived long enough in darkness to know that love, true love, cannot thrive amid dishonesty and falseness.

It was a bitter blow. Just as I had finally gone beyond my past and begun to dream of a future, a major part of what I had dreamed of was taken away from me. And yet I don't – I can't – blame the NHS for this. Who better than I to know that stable, loving homes produce stable, loving children?

Would I have been a good mother? You might have your doubts, but I know just how much love there is inside me: yes, I would be a good mother, just as my mum has been to me. I have learned from the best and seen the worst, so how could I be anything other than a good parent?

All the same, it took me months to come to terms with the realisation that I wasn't going to have a baby. I can't tell you I have got over the loss because I haven't and I don't know that I ever will, but slowly, painfully, I came to terms with it. And I have had help. From Mum – of course – but also from someone new who came into my life. Readers, meet Sula; Sula, meet the readers.

I knew from the moment I saw her that we were meant to be together. She was in Durham, 15 miles away; she lived with her mother and her brothers, and when I first walked into her house our eyes met. She was tiny, a little ball of fluff clambering over her mum and being pushed out of the way by her siblings. I picked her up and she fitted into the palm of my hand.

Because Sula – as you must have guessed – is not a woman, nor even a baby. She is a Shiatsu puppy and taking her home with me – sharing the warmth, the comfort and the love in this little flat – is, quite simply, the best thing I have ever done in my life.

We go everywhere together now; we walk into town together, we curl up on the sofa together and she sleeps at the end of my bed every night. Am I a mother to her, or a big sister? Who knows – and you know what? It doesn't matter. Maybe she's the daughter I would have – should have – had; maybe I am to her the sort of sister I should have been to Rachel. All I know is that what's between us is love.

The name Sula comes from Greece. It was Mum who came up with it: she'd been on holiday there and had met a local girl in a restaurant whose name was Sula. But when I looked into its origins I knew that my little puppy was indeed a Sula: for the name means Peace.

I think now I can answer that question we started with; I think now I understand and I'm ready. What is love? Well, it is many different things and can be found in many different ways. It is in the warm light of a good day, it is in the comfort of true friends.

It is in the caress given by a mother to a child. It is in the hands of someone – anyone – who touches our hands with kindness and our hearts with peace. It is in the long hours of silence when two people share solace and know that the best words are those which never need to be spoken. Love – true, genuine love – is all around us every day; it has existed before we were born and will endure long after we die. But I know this, too: the path to finding love is often hidden or blocked by fear and from fear it is but a short step to a confusion so loud we cannot hear another's call. For most of my life I lived in this state of confusion and fear, unable to hear the love which Mum softly offered.

And love is often usurped by an imposter: sex. I know this and I know it's true: sex, in and of itself, is not love. It can – it often does – pretend to be, but alone and naked it is not love. Only *in* love can sex be loving. Never – ever – can love exist in the same place as grubby commerce, which distorts the hope of true feeling and turns it into a mere physical transaction.

I have escaped from the dark places – both the solid prison bars of sexual slavery and the equally real mental imprisonment of a life lived without love. In those dark places evil flourished and flourishes still: it's name is fear. Fear of the next man to rent my ravaged and abused body. Fear of reprisals – of brutal beatings or worse – should I try to refuse. Fear that ate away at my insides and made me cower and bring myself ever lower and more base as if I could find protection from my abusers in drugs and drink. This is fear; this is evil. I have escaped, but countless thousands of women like me are still there, trapped in the gaudy, tawdry business of selling their bodies.

Will you recognise them, as you recognised me? Will you love and support them as you have cared for me? Or, after this long journey we have shared, will you pass by on the other side, turning your face away and blinding your eyes to what they see?

William Wilberforce, 225 years ago, made a speech in the British Parliament about the evils of slavery and the slave trade. For three long, passionate hours he gave MPs the terrible, brutal truth about an industry that captured human beings and trafficked them across the world as if they were cattle: no – much less than cattle, much less than any living being – as a commodity. He described the suffering and the anguish of this commerce and set out plainly the indifference and the greed which allowed it to flourish. At the end of his speech he said this: 'Having heard all of this you may choose to look the other way. But you can never again say that you did not know.'

Can you – can we – say any longer we do not know the truth about sex slavery? Can any of us say ever again that we are deaf and blind to the stories of women like Katya, Susanna, Mardea – and me?

My name is Sarah Forsyth. I have been many things in my life. I have been an abused child and a sex slave. I have been a crack whore and an alcoholic. I have been in police cells and in prison. I have brought sorrow to my family and failed in my marriage. But I am more, much more than the sum of these things. I have survived the worst men can do to a living body. I have overcome my addictions. I have – finally – made my mum and my sister proud of me. I have, with your help, told a truth about evil and how we can fight it. I am a survivor and I know why.

And the answer is love.

AFTERWORD

It was a bright, clear spring day as I made my way up the little path to Sarah's front door. I had not seen her for more than three years. We had spoken on the phone many times and sent letters back and forth; but as to actually seeing her, face to face, it had been a while.

I was, I confess, slightly nervous. The last time we had been in the same room Sarah had not been in a good way. Then, the day of her wedding, she was still in the grips of her methadone dependency, still addicted to alcohol (and cigarettes), still living with Tracy. It had not been an easy meeting. Sarah was uncomfortable and uneasy, Tracy was watchful. The atmosphere felt tense and overshadowed.

Physically, too, Sarah was frail, her step slow and her face drawn and haunted. Plainly her body was still struggling to cope with the ravages of all she had been through, but I came away equally sure that, whatever her declarations of abiding love for Tracy and happiness in the flat they shared, all was far from well.

In the weeks and months that followed, we worked on Sarah's first book. This, too, proved very difficult. Sarah would often disappear, for days on end, and tracking her down could take huge amounts of time and effort. Her emotions were all over the map: one day she would swear that she adored Tracy and that they were happily, magically, in love; the very next, she would be in floods of tears and describing a fight that had convinced her she hated Tracy and would never, ever go back to her. But of course she did.

I spent almost as much time talking with Sarah's mother, trying to discover if she knew what was going on in her daughter's life and offering what few words of encouragement I could in the face of all the evidence pointing towards yet another meltdown. No, as Sarah herself admitted in the letter preceding my visit that spring morning, it had not been easy.

The initial signs, though, were a bit more promising. On the phone Sarah was bright, clear and very definitely focused. She was determined, she said, not merely to write a second book but to use it – and the influence stemming from *Slave Girl* becoming a bestseller – to do something useful about sex trafficking. Above all, she wanted to make people see the women imprisoned, as she had been, in plain sight; she spoke passionately about wanting readers to know the stories of the sex slaves behind the Red Light District windows or the discretely blackened glass of high street brothels. Because, as she said: 'If people see these women not as sex workers but as human beings – well, they can't fail to care, can they?'

The path up to the house was equally encouraging. Whereas the flat she had shared with Tracy had been in a run-down and shabby inner-city street, here the houses had gardens – neatly kept, all of them – and the paintwork was fresh and clean. The air, too, felt better: less permeated with the smell of kebab bars and chip shops.

Even so, I was utterly unprepared for what happened next. The door was opened by a smart, pretty young woman; her hair neatly styled in a fashionable cut and under her arm a small fluffy dog. I had no idea who this could be and asked if Sarah was at home. She smiled and asked me in. It was, of course, Sarah herself.

The physical difference was astonishing. Sarah's face – once pock-marked and thin with the evidence of her drug and alcohol addiction – had filled out and bloomed. Her eyes no longer alternated between drug-induced sleepiness and fearful wariness; they were warm and twinkled with amusement – not least at my inability to recognise her.

Up a flight of stairs, the cheerfully decorated living room was warm and immediately welcoming. On the sofa, Sarah's long-suffering mother sat, cradling a cup of coffee in her hands. And she, too, was smiling.

Two things were palpably obvious. The relationship between Sarah and her mother – the most important relationship in Sarah's life – was in very good shape indeed. For her part Sarah's mother was clearly proud of her daughter and all she had achieved in a few short years.

And Sarah was proud of her mum: she knew that alone she could never have come this far and that the person – the one person in her life – who had never deserted her, never given up hope, was her mother. Sitting in that cosy living room you might be forgiven for thinking that this was an ordinary mother-daughter relationship, no different to the millions that are played out the length and breadth of the country every day. You would never have thought to see these two vibrant, happy women that one had lost the best years of her adult life to sex slavery and addictions, while the other had endured a decade and a half of constant, draining worry.

The second thing was Sarah's determination that some good would come out of the evil that had engulfed her. It would, I think, have been perfectly understandable for Sarah to have rejoiced in getting her life back, and to have simply got on with the business of enjoying the love of her family. Instead, she was absolutely certain that the journey chronicled in this book was something she had to do. And not for herself.

During the writing of the first book, Sarah's overriding emotions were anger, self-loathing and self-pity. Now, without ever wanting to shrug off what had happened to her – nor, it must be said, to shy away from the decisions she had made which played a part in her ordeal – she felt she had a duty: a responsibility not just to bear witness to what other sex-trafficked women are enduring today and every day, but to do something about the problem itself.

I wondered aloud whether this was altogether a good – or at least a safe – idea. As gently as I could, I asked Sarah if she was really strong enough to go back and face up to the Hell (or, more accurately, the Hells) that had ensnared her. Sarah looked at her mother as she spoke quietly but firmly – she wanted to do this, she needed to do this. And she was going to do this. I looked at her mother, trying to gauge her reaction: she smiled again and nodded her agreement.

But what to do? It's one thing to write a book, even one which – like *Slave Girl* – engendered an almost-universally positive and supporting response from readers, but it's quite another to go from the safety of writing a manuscript to trying to motivate an audience to take action.

At the close of the afternoon we came up with the answer between us and you will find it at the end of this chapter: five suggestions for those of you who feel – as Sarah and I do – that sex slavery and the trafficking which feeds it is too important to ignore. We can't – as William Wilberforce put it – 'choose to look the other way' because we have seen the problem, and once seen, it cannot be forgotten or ignored.

Five hours had passed in animated discussion. As I got up to leave that evening, I knew then how I would end this book.

I have been proud to work with Sarah Forsyth: proud to help her tell her story and to shine a light on a cruel and callous trade in women's bodies, but more than that, I am privileged to know her. Sarah Forsyth, as she says, has been many things in her life but she is a remarkable and brave young woman and I have learned much from her.

I have learned how a body once broken can repair itself.

I have learned how a mind once shattered can heal. And I have learned that the key to these recoveries is the same as the key to unlocking the doors behind which sex slaves are imprisoned. And that key is love.

Thank you, Sarah.

Tim Tate
November 2012

FIVE THINGS YOU CAN DO

1. Take to the streets

Your town – or at least one nearby – will have a brothel. Of course it won't be called that: it will go by the hypocritical euphemism of a 'sauna' or a 'massage parlour'. These businesses have been granted permission to be there and although you can complain to your council, there's probably very little it can do. But there is action you can take – safely and legally.

Assuming these premises are on a public street, you have a perfect right to hand out leaflets to men going in there. Be careful how you word these leaflets – only the police can determine whether there are trafficked women inside. But your leaflets can most certainly ask the question that any 'punter' should ask himself: is there a danger that I could be paying for sex from a woman who is being forced to do this?

This sort of direct action – so long as it is peaceful and non-provocative – can have a real effect. How do we know? Because after an anti-slavery conference Tim attended in the Netherlands, men and women who want to fight sex slavery did almost exactly this in Amsterdam's Red Light District. It didn't put those lights out but it certainly made some would-be customers think twice.

2. Write to your local newspaper
Does your local paper carry adverts for sexual services? These will invariably be placed towards the back pages and may go under the euphemism 'adult services'. They will advertise 'saunas', 'massage parlours' and 'escort services'.

One leading newspaper group – Newsquest – has already adopted a policy of refusing these adverts. And, as we've seen, the Metropolitan Police have warned others against doing so.

Letters to your local newspaper, protesting about these fronts for prostitution, can make a difference.

3. Write to your MP asking for a change in the Law
Britain's prostitution laws are a mess – which is one reason why pimps and traffickers find it relatively easy to operate here. It is not a criminal offence for a woman to sell sexual services but it is an offence to solicit for customers (most usually taken to mean street-walking), and it is also against the law to operate a brothel – which is the other most likely way for a woman to practise prostitution. The net result is that women run the risk of arrest for selling sex.

There's a far more sensible way forward. Instead of

criminalising the woman – who may well have been forced into sex slavery – why not make it a criminal offence for anyone to pay for sex? Sweden already has this law and, as we've seen, it appears to be working. As we write, the parliaments in Northern Ireland and Scotland are considering bringing in exactly this sort of legislation. But England and Wales – which collectively have a far higher number of brothels – are not. Write to your MP asking him or her to support, or even put forward, a change in the Law.

4. Write to airlines and holiday companies

Sex is big business – and not just for the pimps. Just about every airline flies groups of passengers to cities like Amsterdam, Prague, Budapest and Thailand on what amount to sex tours.

The airlines don't officially know that these are what they are – even though it can painfully obvious, given the now-standard printed T-shirts bearing the words 'So and so's Amsterdam Red Light Tour 2012'.

While it may be good business for the airlines, very few – if any – would want to be seen to be making profits out of sex slavery. Write to the airlines asking them not to stop flying but instead to include a hand-out to every adult passenger heading for known prostitution tourism, warning that many women they will encounter may have been trafficked and forced into selling their bodies.

Holiday companies are often more brazen. The popularity of foreign stag weekends has led to package tours of the more (in)famous Red Light District. It's not against the Law, but just as with airlines, shouldn't the tour operators take some responsibility? After all, they're making money from this misery. Write to them, too, asking them to include warning flyers about the prevalence of sex slavery in these Red Light zones.

5. Ask for help – and to help
There are several very good and dedicated charities working to end sex slavery. Ask them for advice and information – they'll be only too happy to hear from you. And they'll be especially pleased if you offer your help with their next campaign.

Tim has worked extensively with the following groups and knows just how dedicated they are to protecting women trapped in sex slavery – and attacking the organisations and mechanisms that traffick them there.

RESOURCES

NOT FOR SALE
http://www.notforsalecampaign.org

Not For Sale fights human trafficking and modern-day slavery around the world. Through international work on the ground and in mainstream supply chains, it proactively targets the root causes of slavery, while engaging and equipping the movement for freedom.

Its European headquarters is based in Amsterdam, where Toos Heemskirk – the woman we met earlier – works to help and protect the sex slaves trapped in prostitution. It also has a pioneering self-help operation in Romania, which seeks both to prevent women from being lured into international sex slavery and to support this who have escaped from it.

Not For Sale has also developed a unique consumer tool

for use in the fight against slave-made goods in our shops. It's a free downloadable 'App' for Smartphones: point it at a product with a barcode and you'll get a report on how much effort the manufacturer is making to prevent slavery in its workplace. We strongly recommend this as a great and important tool for everyone.

FREE THE SLAVES
https://www.freetheslaves.net

Free The Slaves has a clear, straightforward goal: to end slavery in our lifetime. Everything it does is weighed against one simple question: will this free slaves and help them stay free?

Led by Kevin Bales – the world's leading authority on modern slavery – it works actively to free slaves around the world by teaming up with grassroots organisations in countries where slavery flourishes. It also records and shares the stories of slaves so that people in power can see slavery and be inspired to work for freedom.

Free The Slaves is non-political and non-partisan. It works with governments to produce effective anti-slavery laws then holds them to their commitments. And it researches what works and what doesn't so that resources are strategically and effectively used to end slavery. For ever.

ANTI-SLAVERY INTERNATIONAL
www.antislavery.org

Founded in 1839, Anti-Slavery International is the world's oldest international human rights organisation and the only charity in the United Kingdom to work exclusively against slavery and related abuses.

Anti-Slavery International lobbies governments of countries with slavery to act against it and to increase the priority of combating slavery. It also funds and helps solid scientific research to find out the extent of modern slavery and passes that on to the public. Quite simply, its goal is a world without slaves.

THE A21 CAMPAIGN
http://www.thea21campaign.org

Borne of a simple belief that 'someone should do something' about sex slavery, The A21 Campaign does just that. At the end of 2008, it opened its first shelter for victims of human trafficking in Greece.

Through the shelter and transition home, it is able to provide trafficked victims with a safe, loving and comforting environment, access to medical care and psychological assessment, vocational training, assistance in university education, life guidance and counselling, and access to legal assistance. A21 works closely with police, hospitals and government officials, and is seeing justice enjoyed by new rescued victims each month.

In 2011, it opened its second transition home in

Ukraine. Because Ukraine is one of the largest exporters of women into the international sex industry, the A21 team is focusing efforts on preventing human trafficking before it happens, through school tours, working with orphanages and education.

The shelters run by A21 are full of young women who have been freed from a life of bondage. And that has to be a good thing. As the Campaign says: 'Anyone can join. Everyone can make a difference.'

Remember, though: never take the law into your own hands. We can – together – write the wrongs of sex slavery and sex trafficking but never, ever by being in the wrong ourselves.

And finally, both Sarah and Tim would like to hear from you. If you have comments or questions please contact us at: forsythslavegirl@gmail.com.

Thank you for reading, thank you for caring and thank you for your love and support.